A Murder Most Foul!

Or, A Time to Cry;
A Time to Die

Stanley J. Marks

Introduction by Rob Couteau
Afterword by James DiEugenio

DOMINANTSTAR

First published 2023 by Dominantstar LLC, New York.

ISBN 978-1-7360049-7-5

First edition. 1 2 3 4 5 6 7 8 9 10 01

Special thanks to James DiEugenio, Bobbie Marks, Len Osanic, Al Rossi, and Yongzhen Zhang.

Cover: Photo of President Kennedy with his son taken on October 10, 1963, about a month before his assassination. Credit: Cecil Stoughton. John F. Kennedy Presidential Library and Museum, Boston.

Contents

John F. Kennedy and family, 1963. (Unknown photographer.) From the Jim Wright Collection, Weatherford College, accessed at the online Portal to Texas History.

"I knew President Kennedy through his book *Profiles in Courage*. I knew him from the statements he made, first as a presidential candidate, and then as President of the Republic, and I knew him from his inaugural address. I was unprepared to find a young man who had a universal concept of his functions as the head of the United States government and who saw Latin American problems from a point of view that, in my judgment, no other American chief of state has had. This was my personal impression of the rare, I repeat, almost unprecedented case of a man who did not represent the abstract concept of the State, but who imparted a new dimension to the governing function, and that dimension, in my opinion, was the result of his sensitivity: a rare, very masculine, very virile sensitivity. I would say that President Kennedy loved his country, the United States, as if the United States had been really a physical being, his mother, father, or older brother. And he had a guilt complex about what the United States may have done to the detriment of other countries in the past.... When I met President Kennedy, I found myself in the presence of a human being far more intense than I had expected – a type of chief of state never before known, I believe, in United States history, and perhaps even in the history of Europe, perhaps in the Western world, since the days of Greece; there may have been a few like him, but not in modern times, because the head of government usually places the interests of the State above his personality and his personal feelings. He represents an abstract value, which is the State. In my judgment, this was not true in President Kennedy's case. He tried to rectify all the damage the United States may have caused and to create a new image of his country. And this profound identification, so deeply felt, between a head of state and his people had never before occurred, I believe, in the history of his country, not even in the case of Abraham Lincoln.... This impression was created not only by what he said, but by his attitude. He was a man whose attitude was one of compassion, something that was hardly to be expected between a citizen of the United States and a citizen of the Dominican Republic or of Africa. I should mention that, in our conversation, during the many points we discussed, there was a moment when we spoke of the war danger, and, at that moment, President Kennedy reacted as if war, the idea that war could reach America – not the United States, but Latin America – pained him personally. It hurt him as much as it could hurt me, a Latin American.... In the course of an hour and fifteen minutes of conversation, President Kennedy had said nothing that was not in defense of the Dominican people, or the Dominican Republic, either from the point of view of Dominican national policy or from the Dominican international point of view vis-à-vis the American policy. He spent the entire time that he talked to me defending the Dominican Republic. That is to say, it seemed that the one who was talking was not he, but myself, and this impressed me greatly.... We spoke among other things of the state-owned enterprises, the companies that had belonged to the Trujillo family. President Kennedy offered me all kinds of technical and other assistance in order to prevent those companies from being sold to private individuals, and especially to American companies. If it should some become necessary to sell them owing to a lack of technical know-how or capital in my country, it would be preferable that they not be sold to American interest. But he was in favor of not selling those companies. The kind of general assistance that President Kennedy offered me for the development of the Dominican Republic and not for the benefit of the United States, was generous, and, moreover, that help was actually given to such an extent that American officials – and this you know – even went to offer assistance to the Dominican Government.... There have been two great presidents in the United States who have thoroughly understood Latin America. One was called Abraham Lincoln. His attitude during the invasion of Mexico was that of a Latin American leader. The other was John Fitzgerald Kennedy.... President Kennedy was fighting for the right of the masses, the unknown man, not as a politician who wanted to avoid conflicts in his country, but as a man of the people who wanted to put culture and prosperity within reach of the common man. President Kennedy and President Lincoln were the only presidents who were two things at the same time: ruler and common man. Such a phenomenon is seldom seen in history."

– Juan Bosch, Oral History Interview, June 9, 1964, John F. Kennedy Library Oral History Program. Bosch was the first democratically elected president of the Dominican Republic. He was later overthrown by the CIA under Kennedy's successor, President Lyndon Baines Johnson.

Burial of President Kennedy at Arlington National Cemetery. Photo credit: Abbie Rowe, John F. Kennedy Presidential Library and Museum, Boston.

President Kennedy meets with former President Harry S. Truman, January 21, 1961. Photo credit: Abbie Rowe, John F. Kennedy Presidential Library and Museum, Boston.

The Ripple Effect: An Introduction to Stanley J. Marks' Three-act Play about the JFK Assassination

Barbara Garson's *MacBird!*, a satire based on *Macbeth* that borrows lines from Shakespeare, was the first widely publicized play about the JFK assassination. Privately printed in 1966, the playscript was reissued by both Penguin and Grove the following year, eventually selling over 200,000 copies. After opening at Manhattan's Village Gate in February 1967, it was produced in Los Angeles – the adopted home of Stanley Marks – and at the Committee Theater in San Francisco.

As a devoted assassination researcher and connoisseur of theater, it's likely that Stan Marks witnessed at least one performance of *MacBird!* during its long run. We can also assume that he was outraged by its cynical, insipid treatment of the Kennedy legacy, which portrayed the most empathy-driven president as being "heartless." Garson even has Robert Kennedy (as "Robert Ken O'Dunc") declaim that this "heartless" state was deliberately arranged by his own father:

> To free his sons from paralyzing scruples
> And temper us for roles of world authority
> Our pulpy human hearts were cut away. [...]
> And so, MacBird, that very man you fear,
> Your heartless, bloodless foe now lifts his spear.[1]

Thus, in a bizarre inversion of actual events, the scene portrays Robert as the murderer of President Johnson ("MacBird") in a cold-blooded act that he tries to cover up. Garson also had the

---

[1] Barbara Garson, *The Complete Text of MacBird!*, New York: Grove Press, 1967, p. 107.

An example of how the corporate mass media selectively presents the news: "(New Orleans) — A witness at the Clay Shaw conspiracy trial in New Orleans has told of hearing three or four shots fired at the time President Kennedy was killed. Robert West, a Texas land surveyor, testified he heard four reports, the first similar to motorcycle backfire and three others like rifle fire." Note how this statement is neatly aligned with the official story: of three bullets fired, supposedly from Oswald's gun. The editor's pencil then crosses out the following paragraph, which would have turned things upside down. Excised from their report: "District Attorney Jim Garrison said at the outset of the trial that the president was struck by bullets fired from different guns at different places. The Warren Commission report said that one gunman Lee Oswald shot Kennedy from behind."

The National Broadcasting Network (NBC) was notorious for its blatant attacks against Jim Garrison, but behind the scenes it often engaged in more subtle methods. We now know that the network was at the forefront of the CIA's secret and carefully coordinated campaign to sully Garrison's reputation.

Source: "WBAP-TV, Fort Worth, Texas. News script: Clay Shaw Conspiracy Trial." February 13, 1969. KXAS-NBC 5 News Collection, University of North Texas Libraries Special Collections, accessed at The Portal to Texas History, texashistory.unt.edu.

temerity to remark that if President Johnson had helped to assassinate JFK (a point of view that she didn't necessarily advocate) it would have been "the least of his crimes."[2]

---

[2] And if anyone has any doubts about JFK's remarkable empathy, this eloquent statement made by his wife four months after the assassination should put them to rest: "Just as an example of him having a heart – I can remember him being so disgusted, because once we had dinner with my mother and my stepfather, and there sat my stepfather putting a great slab of paté de foie gras on his toast and saying it was simply appalling to think that the minimum wage should be a dollar twenty-five. And Jack saying to me when we went home, 'Do you realize that those laundrywomen in the South get sixty cents an hour?' Or sixty cents a day, or whatever it was. And how horrified he was when he saw General Eisenhower – President Eisenhower, I guess – in their Camp David meeting before inauguration – and Eisenhower had said to him – they were talking about the Cuban refugees – and Eisenhower said, 'Of course, they'd be so great if you could just ship a lot of them up in trucks from Miami and use 'em as servants for twenty dollars a month, but I suppose somebody'd raise a fuss if you tried to do that.' You know, again, so appalled at all these rich people just thinking of how you can live on – not thinking how you can live on just twenty dollars a month, but just to use these people like slaves. He was just so hurt for them, though he'd say it in a sentence [....] And then, another time, when you were trying to raise money for the cultural center, and a Republican friend of my stepfather said, 'Why don't you get labor to do it? If you took a dollar a week out of all of labor's wages, you could have the money raised in no time at all.' And he was just really sickened by that and said, 'Can you think what a dollar a week out of their wages would mean to all those people?' So all those things show that he did have a heart, because he was really shocked by those things." Interviewer Arthur M. Schlesinger, Jr. adds: "Of course, he had a heart, [but] it wasn't on his sleeve ... But he was deeply affected." See Jacqueline Kennedy, *Historic Conversations on Life with John F. Kennedy*, New York: Hyperion, 2011, p. 66-67. Jacqueline also recalled a telling incident

Perhaps as a response to all this Marks decided to write his own play: one informed by far greater insight into the actual case. He never lost sight of the fact that the forces that reaped untold financial profits with Johnson at the helm were the same ones that had removed JFK and plunged the nation into a turmoil from which it has never recovered. But none of this is even hinted at in Garson's drama, which soon received blessings from major media outlets, including approving reviews in the *New York Times*, the *Washington Post*, the *New York Review of Books*, and the *Chicago Daily News*.

While Garson and her reviewers were focused on the animosity flaring between Robert Kennedy and Lyndon Johnson (an example of what Joan Didion derisively refers to as the "sentimental narrative" that passes as American "journalism"), Marks was asking questions about the true nature of mass media and about its infiltration by embedded CIA agents. Such inquiries were rarely posed in 1967, the year that he published his first assassination inquiry, also titled *Murder Most Foul!* and subtitled *The Conspiracy That Murdered President Kennedy: 975 Questions & Answers*.

That text appeared in September 1967, five months before he copyrighted his play on February 19, 1968. The questions raised,

---

involving Robert Kennedy. When the CIA failed to protect Oleg Penkovsky, a secret agent in Moscow who was arrested and executed, RFK approached Jacqueline, "just looking so sad ... and he said, 'It's just awful, they don't have any heart at CIA. They just think of everyone there as a number. He's Spy X-15.' And he said that he'd said to them, you know, 'Why? This man was just feeding you too many hot things. He was just bound to get caught. And they'd keep asking him for more. Why didn't someone warn him? Why didn't someone tell him to get out? He has a family. A wife or children or something.' Bobby was just so wounded by them – just treating that man like a cipher.'" Ibid., pp. 192-93.

the evidence gathered, and the jigsaw puzzle assembled in his first JFK book (MMF-1) were still fresh in his mind when he tackled his playscript, "A Murder Most Foul! Or, A Time to Cry; A Time to Die" (MMF-2). And so, it remains of interest to compare these two works and to see how, in the play, he focuses on several of the more salient points raised in his nonfiction, now lending them an alternate form of expression via the dialogue of various characters.

For example, in MMF-1, Stanley writes: "That the CIA controls many of the news columns in both the press and magazines is now known. What is not known, and what will never be known, is how many agents of the CIA now work for various organs in the mass communication media."

In MMF-2 we witness the following dialogue that occurs between King (a leading backer of the plot) and his henchmen, Noslen and Prince, as they discuss Oswald in relationship to the assassination of Patrolman Tippit and the attempted murder of Major General Edwin Walker:

> NOSLEN: From the television and other newspaper reports published last year, there seems to be no doubt that Patsy was the only one involved in those affairs.
>
> KING: Let me say that those reports were made by organizations who know on what side their bread is buttered.

And later in the play:

> KING: And the owners of the press didn't give a damn and they still don't give a damn. In fact, I

would venture a guess that ninety percent of them
applauded his [JFK's] murder.

Stanley continually reminds us that one of the greatest weapons
at the disposal of the American Empire is a brainwashed populace. For how else can the Establishment continue to finance,
without serious objection, its illegal wars of conquest, both
economic and political?

Like the first MMF, the play also pokes fun at the absurdities
put forth by the Warren Commission. For example, MMF-1
hosts a chapter titled "Rifles, Rifles, Everywhere," referring to
the fact that, shortly after the assassination, police discovered
more than one firearm in the Texas School Book Depository,
and the press published photos of more than one type of
Mannlicher-Carcano rifle in the hands of police. (Besides that
infamously dilapidated, rusty old Mannlicher-Carcano that FBI
investigators initially refused to test, for fear it would explode
in their faces, there was also a more sophisticated weapon: a
7.65 German Mauser.) Marks explores this same set of facts in
MMF-2 with a scene that's also titled "Rifles, Rifles,
Everywhere." But this entire episode now occurs in silence,
minus any dialogue, with only one character, who conducts a
"dry run" of the murder using two rifles, each with telescopic
sights. Fittingly enough, the weapons are hidden in golf bags.

Pause for a moment to linger over this potent symbol. For me,
it calls to mind how President Eisenhower, who mollycoddled
the CIA and allowed it to mushroom to gigantic proportions as
it assumed autonomous powers in the 1950s (one of Kennedy's
aides even called it a "state within a state"),[3] was known as the

---

[3] After noting "the autonomy with which the agency has been permitted to operate," Arthur Schlesinger, Jr. warned President Kennedy:
"The contemporary CIA possesses many of the characteristics of a

president who "brought golf to the White House lawn." During his tenure there, Eisenhower carded over eight-hundred rounds of this leisurely activity while the CIA was busy overthrowing democratically elected governments around the world. Thus, how fitting that King stuffs a box of bullets into a pouch on the bag that's normally reserved for golf balls!

Marks may or may not have consciously drawn this connection to Eisenhower, but in his stage direction for this scene he includes an even more overt symbol: "On the mantelpiece, centered, is a large derrick, painted or glazed in gold. At the top of the derrick is a small Confederate flag." This clearly alludes the Texas oil cabal that would have rejoiced over the president's death, especially because JFK wanted to end the oil depletion allowance: the largest tax loophole in American history. But the derrick also points to that "bigger picture" perspective that Marks has always assumed: that, beyond the theatrical stage of Dealey Plaza, one must also investigate the money trail leading to corporate interests and their role in changing the course of history.

Later in the play, in a wonderful cross-pollination with nonfiction, King uses a slide projector to display Deputy Sheriff Weitzman's affidavit, which testifies to the fact that Weitzman discovered a German Mauser inside the Texas School Book Depository. But of course, Weitzman was later compelled to alter his testimony to match a new "script," now claiming that the rifle in question must have been an Italian Mannlicher-Carcano all along. This despite the fact that he was a firearms

---

state within a state." Arthur Schlesinger, Jr., "CIA Reorganization" memo to President Kennedy, June 30, 1961, p. 3. (For more on this memo, see my essay "On the Life and Times of Stanley J. Marks," below.)

expert who would never have made such a foolish error. But just as a playwright wouldn't hesitate to alter a first draft, the Warren Commission report was always a fictional "work in progress." One of the classic lines in Stanley's drama sums this up rather nicely:

> Prince: At least the Commission was consistent; it started and finished with lies.

This is not the sort of thing that one would encounter in a mainstream media-endorsed drama about the assassination – especially back in 1968. And what other playwright from that era would include the following "Notes to producer and director":

> In Act II, Scene I, two false Oswalds are seen but not heard. There is more than sufficient evidence in the report and the hearings to prove that, in the conspiracy, a minimum of three Oswalds were used.

The scene that follows depicts "Executor," the leader of a hit team, interacting with his ruthless subordinates Lion, Hawk, and Bulldog:

> (LION walks to rear right door, opens it, and motions with hand. In walk two men, dressed in the identical clothes worn by MARINE, hair combed the same way, and the same height and build. They walk only about ten feet into room, stop and face the others.)
>
> CUBANS: It can't be! Three of them! What's up?

EXECUTOR: Yes, these two men look like Marine. They are decoys chosen to protect us and him. At no time will anyone of you speak to any one of them unless they speak to you first. That's an order!

(EXECUTOR waves his hand to the two new actors who turn and walk out of door, closing it behind them.)

Speaking of Oswald look-alikes,[4] this might be the place to examine Marks' ideas about Oswald as seen through the evolution of his oeuvre. Marks has always maintained a fluid position regarding the two classic schools of thought about this former marine who, in the words of Senator Schweiker, "had the fingerprints of Intelligence all over him."

On the one hand, we have the notion that Oswald was manip- ulated into assuming an active role in the assassination.

On the other hand, we have the possibility that he was simply chosen to be an unwitting patsy who could be tricked into shouldering the blame for the president's murder.

Throughout his nonfiction Marks has always leaned more toward the patsy position, though he adds that, as an attorney, he cannot definitively discount the other possibility simply because we don't have all the evidence at our disposal. Thus, I was surprised to learn that, in the drama, Marks inserts Marine directly into a group that plans and executes the assassination.

---

[4] Tenacious researchers have continued to plumb the depths of this mystery ever since the appearance of Richard Popkin's *The Second Oswald* (New York: Avon Books, 1966), a text cited by Stanley in MMF-1.

AFFIDAVIT IN ANY FACT

THE STATE OF TEXAS
COUNTY OF DALLAS

BEFORE ME, Mary Rattan

a Notary Public in and for said County, State of Texas, on this day personally appeared.

Seymour Weitzman w/m, 2802 Oates Drive, DA7 6624. Bus. Roble Love, RI1 1483

Who, after being by me duly sworn, on oath deposes and says: Yesterday November 22, 1963 I was standing on the corner of Main and Houston, and as the President passed and made his turn going west towards Stemmons, I walked casually around. At this time my partner was behind me and asked me something. I looked back at him and heard 3 shots. I ran in a northwest direction and scaled a fence towards where we thought the shots came from. Then someone said they thought the shots came from the old Texas Building. I immediately ran to the Texas Building and started looking inside. At this time Captain Fritz arrived and ordered all of the sixth floor sealed off and searched. I was working with Deputy S. Boone of the Sheriff's Department and helping in the search. We were in the northwest corner of the sixth floor when Deputy Boone and myself spotted the rifle about the same time. This rifle was a 7.65 Mauser bolt action equipped with a 4/18 scope, a thick leather brownish-black sling on it. The rifle was between some boxes near the stairway. The time the rifle was found was 1:22 pm. Captain Fritz took charge of the rifle and ejected one live round from the chamber. I then went back to the office after this.

Seymour Weitzman

SUBSCRIBED AND SWORN TO BEFORE ME THIS 23 DAY OF November A.D. 1963

Mary Rattan Mary Rattan
Notary Public, Dallas County, Texas

CPS-OF-413

Deputy Sheriff Weitzman's affidavit reads, in part: "We were in the northwest corner of the sixth floor when Deputy Boone and myself spotted the rifle about the same time. This rifle was a 7.65 Mauser bolt action equipped with a 4/18 scope, a thick leather brownish black sling on it. The rifle was between some boxes near the stairway. The time the rifle was found was 1:22 p.m. Captain Fritz took charge of the rifle and ejected one live round from the chamber."

Source: "Affidavit in Any Fact – Statement by Seymour Weitzman, November 23, 1963 #1." John F. Kennedy, Dallas Police Department Collection, provided by the Dallas Municipal Archives and accessed at The Portal to Texas History.

Marine / Oswald is told that he's to serve as a "decoy," and he plays no role in the shooting. But he's referred to as "Patsy" behind his back, as the plotter's have earmarked him to take the fall.

But a careful reading of the play opens up another possibility regarding Marine's true role:

When Prince asks King if "Patsy" was either an FBI informant or a CIA agent, after carefully defining the term "agent" King confirms that Patsy served in both these roles:

> Look at Patsy's record. He was ordered to learn the Russian language while he was a Marine. He was trained at a Japanese airfield as an agent. He was ordered to Russia as an agent while he was still in the Inactive Reserve and retained his Class A Marine security clearance. He returned and again acted his part as a Red and Bearded One [Castro] sympathizer. He operated a one-man pro-Bearded One committee out of a room next door to an EIA-controlled agency [the CIA]. He was subject to arrest when he returned from Russia, yet no federal agency made the arrest. Why?

This represents a view that the author consistently held throughout his nonfiction work. As early as 1967, in MMF-1 Marks asks: "Who was Lee Harvey Oswald?" Answer: "Evidence is now accumulating that he was a minor cog in the CIA." He continues: "Was Oswald any type of Agent for the CIA?" "The evidence is accumulating that the answer is 'yes.'" "Was Oswald either an FBI agent or informer?" "Yes, as to being an informant, as distinguished from being an agent." In his next nonfiction book, *Two Days of Infamy: November 22, 1963; September 28, 1964* (1969), he adds that even if Oswald was "part and parcel of the conspiracy" he represents no more than a "piece of string [tied] around the conspiracy package." And in *Coup d'État! Three Murders That Changed the Course of History. President Kennedy, Reverend King, Senator R. F. Kennedy* (1970), he further refines this view:

> ... a conspiracy murdered President Kennedy; but whether Oswald was a part of the conspiracy cannot be ascertained. Under the "basic principles of American justice," if a person enters into a conspiracy to commit murder, and the murder is committed, then the degree of the participation is of no consequence – that person is guilty of the full penalty. If, however, a person takes some action of which he has no knowledge that his action is part of a conspiracy, he cannot be guilty of any crime. There is evidence that Oswald was used as a "patsy"; that he executed a part of the conspiracy but he had no knowledge of what was to occur.

In the playscript we have a patsy who is fully cognizant of the upcoming assassination and who also serves as an FBI informant and CIA asset. This leads to the question: Is Marine reporting back to either bureau about the plan to murder the chief of state, perhaps trying to prevent it? And what sort of follow-up orders is he receiving from his handlers in these respective agencies? The author doesn't tell us; and so, the mystery of Marine remains intact, lending the drama a more resonant, intentional ambiguity.

But we are offered a clue about Marine's own execution. Executor has decided that Marine must be eliminated, because he can't be trusted to remain silent:

> Do you think the Department has forgotten that he tried to commit suicide, and failed, while in Russia? He will crack wide open. You don't think for a minute that we would let him go on trial? How asinine do you think we are? Oh, he will play his part to perfection, but to us he is nothing more than our great, big, beautiful patsy. And in this game, as you know, Lion, the only good patsy is a dead one.

The Oswald episode also features a droll exhibition of Marksian wit. In early radio broadcasts of Marine's arrest, Stanley has police officials refer to Marine as "P. Patsy." The solemn tone of these announcements, which otherwise read like actual transcripts from November twenty-second, make the reference to a "Mr. Patsy" seem all the more surreal. One can also imagine the playwright giving us a sly wink when we learn that a radio host even bears the same name as the author: "Stan."

By comparing Marks' nonfiction to his dramatic work we witness the power of dialogue, of the spoken word, to enunciate complex ideas in a highly condensed, direct fashion. Whether MMF-2 works as a successful play that will rivet an audience's attention is another question entirely. Such a didactic scenario is faced with numerous challenges, as the presentation of *ideas* (rather than the dramatization of a character's shifting *emotions*) serves as its primary spine. Stanley even alludes to this in his stage direction when he writes: "The play can thus deal only in fact and the characters are subordinate to the main theme of the play, which reveals the methods used to murder President John F. Kennedy; why he was murdered; and how his murder

City of Dallas
OFFICE MEMORANDUM

To- Chief Stevenson
Capt Fritz

Subject: Information on threats on President
Kennedy

The wife of Detective R. E. Abbott said that a former employee
at Parkland hospital was heard by Mrs. Johnson on the admission
desk and a orderly named HOSEY saying that President Kennedy
would be killed. The former employee was a Cuban.

His name can be furnished by Mr. Morgan, who is Mrs Abbotts
supervisor.

O. A. Jones
Captain of Police

The only reason you and I are here is to assist the people of Dallas

Among the many unexplained events of November 22, 1963 we have this Dallas Police Department memo from Captain Jones to Chief Stevenson and Captain Fritz, which bears the heading "Subject: Information on threats on President Kennedy." It reads: "The wife of Detective R. E. Abbott said that a former employee at Parkland hospital was heard by Mrs. Johnson on the admission desk and an orderly named HOSEY saying that President Kennedy would be killed. The former employee was a Cuban. His name can be furnished by Mr. Morgan, who is Mrs. Abbott's supervisor."

Source: "Memorandum concerning threats against President John F. Kennedy, November 22, 1963." John F. Kennedy, Dallas Police Department Collection, accessed at The Portal to Texas History.

changed the course of history." But as a text that presents the keynotes of the assassination, it remains fascinating.

The various characters also personify broader social tendencies. For instance, Noslen is appropriately named because he fails to see things that are right under his nose. In contrast, King possesses a sort of royal sagacity as well as an ability to wed logic to common sense. He's even able to adduce evidence for a conspiracy merely by examining the daily press. And King is a "kingmaker" thanks to his leading role in the plot.

The characters also give voice to some of the principal notions of the author, who often speaks directly to us via King and Prince. (At one point, Prince even says that he's an attorney, just like Stanley.)

> PRINCE: My God, this is worse than *Alice in Wonderland*.

> KING: No, more like Orwell's *1984*. The worst is yet to come.

King is speaking about the revelations he's about to unveil regarding the assassination and its cover-up, but he could just as easily be referring to what will happen after Kennedy's demise: the resumption of a Cold War sensibility once this radical change of government arrives via coup d'état. And Marks would not have been surprised to learn that the cover-up continues to this day, with thousands of assassination-related documents still being illegally held under lock and key – not to mention files that are "missing," illegible, or destroyed. But he holds out a sliver of hope that, eventually, at least part of the truth will emerge. This involves not only an understanding of

Dealey Plaza events but also a macro view regarding the financial interests of transnational corporations:

> KING: [...] We may be able to keep the reasons why the chief was murdered from our generation. However, sometime in the future, students of the event will finally discover the fact that he was done away with because our group believed that the chief's conduct of our national and international affairs was inimical to both us and the nation. Another man said it in another manner: What was good for GM was good for the nation. Just as he placed his interests first, so do we.

Executor voices similar concerns:

> We have discovered that the chief has sent a secret agent to open negotiations with the Bearded One [Fidel Castro]. He is attempting a détente with the Reds. His feelers with the various Red nations to obtain some sort of peace, a "live and let live" attitude, does not appeal to us and to various sectors of our economy. Internally, there's too damn much socialism. So, we believe he must go, and go he will.

As with Marks' nonfiction, such statements transcend a microanalysis of the assassination (e.g., how many bullets were fired; where was Oswald when JFK was shot) and expand into a broader perspective of what was really behind it. Sometimes, this is rendered in a single sentence:

KING: [...] Mr. Noslen, do you think we will ever get out of Vietnam?

We also have this startling remark made by King, shortly after Patsy's assassination:

> You know, when I organized this event, I never thought the ramifications would be so great ... I found that a conspiracy is like throwing a stone in the water. From the center, the ripples keep getting larger and larger until it seems that the whole body of water is agitated. Everything those ripples touch reacts in a different manner. We murdered one man today, but a thousand, no, hundreds of thousands are going to die. No one on this earth will ever be the same.

This climactic statement captures the central concept of the play and transforms it into a highly condensed, potent simile. When we place this illuminating dialogue into the context of what will occur in places such as the Congo, Indonesia, and Vietnam as a result of a radical shift away from JFK's anticolonialist policies, we realize that it can be read as an understatement. For, *millions upon millions* of were indeed killed in paramilitary operations that were essentially vast programs of extermination.[5] Thus, by

---

[5] When I asked JFK historian James DiEugenio for a rough estimate of how many were killed as a result of Kennedy's policies being reversed, he replied: Vietnam: 5.8 million, and this includes the Cambodian Holocaust. Indonesia: a low estimate is 500K; a high estimate would be 850K. Congo: usually given as 100K, but, after the overthrow of Mobutu, the number exploded to well over five million." Private communication with DiEugenio, December 24, 2023. See also Greg

fashioning such pithily rendered phrases, Marks is utilizing the full power of dialogue to condense and yet amplify such ideas, some of which are prescient.

Marks also extends the scope of the play by examining things not normally associated with a JFK assassination chronicle. For example, Ronald Reagan appears here, thinly disguised as "Hameger," the "governor of Khalif" (California). King reminds us that

> The governor of Khalif's approach to Vietnam was to make a parking lot out of North Vietnam. In other words, his Christian approach was the complete extermination of approximately eight million men, women, and children. [...]

Poulgrain, *JFK vs Allen Dulles: Battleground Indonesia* (2020) and Richard D. Mahoney, *JFK: Ordeal in Africa* (1983). There were also dire consequences in Latin America: "I believe that if President Kennedy had remained in office for eight years, he would have left a tradition of political unity between the two Americas, of working together. It did not happen that way. The fatal bullet did much harm to you, but greater harm to us." Juan Bosch, former president of the Dominican Republic, interviewed by Lloyd Cutler, June 9, 1964, p. 15; John F. Kennedy Library Oral History Program. Cf. Robert F. Kennedy's famous "Ripple of Hope" address at the University of Capetown, South Africa, on June 6, 1966: "Each time a man stands up for an ideal, or acts to improve the lot of others, or strikes out against injustice, he sends forth a tiny ripple of hope, and crossing each other from a million different centers of energy and daring those ripples build a current which can sweep down the mightiest walls of oppression and resistance." The first half of the quote is engraved on RFK's memorial at Arlington National Cemetery.

The North Vietnam are all dead, and you have
used their blood, bones, and muscles to mix with
the cement that made the parking lot. Now, what
do you use it for?

Indeed, Governor Reagan once infamously remarked: "It's silly
talking about how many years we will have to spend in the
jungles of Vietnam when we could pave the whole country and
put parking stripes on it and still be home for Christmas."
Marks rightfully equates this with a policy of extermination.
Even after Reagan became president (an event that Marks
predicts in this play, a dozen years before it occurred), Reagan
never renounced such disturbing views.

The grim imagery of this scene in which "blood, bones, and
muscles" are amalgamated with "the cement that made the
parking lot" resonates with another set of dark images that
appear later, in Act III. Although Marks doesn't draw a direct
line between these two points in the drama, the language employed connects them. In this latter scene, he portrays a chaplain addressing American troops in Vietnam from a pulpit on
the battlefield:

Oh, Lord, our God, I summon your help for the
mighty task you have imposed upon your soldiers.
That task of crushing those who believe not in
your words. [...] May we have the strength to use
our weapons of flame to burn, to ground into dust
the bodies of all those who refuse our command
that they give unto thee their loyalty and devotion.
May our weapons make the soil unfertile; the
women to cease childbearing; the blood, bones,
and sinews of the men ground into the dust as

your punishment for their defiance of your holy command.

The hypocrisy of praying to God for one's success in committing barbaric atrocities has rarely been captured with such bitter, acerbic irony. And all this belongs in a play about the assassination, because what's also being portrayed here is what will occur after Kennedy's policies are reversed by President Johnson.[6]

* * *

Perhaps the most unusual tack that Marks takes in this dramatic journey is to introduce a buyer's remorse into the mind of the main protagonist. By allowing King to question whether the assassins did more harm than good, Marks is able to shift the focus of the play to a new point: the snowballing of cynicism in the American psyche, the increasing distrust in government, and the incremental annulment of the American Dream, all of which are rooted in the events of November twenty-second. A debate over this topic that plays out between

---

[6] In this regard, certain remarks made by Jacqueline Kennedy proved to be rather farsighted. As early as June 2, 1964, speaking about Laos and Vietnam, she said: "Jack always said the political thing there was more important than the military, and nobody's thinking of that. And they don't call the people who were in it before [back] in. And so that's the way chaos starts. If you read the story of the Bay of Pigs in the papers now, I mean, the CIA just operating so in the dark, saying, 'Even if you get an order from the president, go ahead with it.' Well, that's the kind of thing that's going to happen again." Jacqueline Kennedy, *Historic Conversations on Life with John F. Kennedy*, pp. 272-73.

King, Prince, and Noslen reaches its culmination in Act III, and it foreshadows the final action in the drama.

But is King's "character shift" artfully accomplished? It appears to arrive out of "left" field, and one might argue that the author has failed to convincingly foreshadow such a result. But setting this reservation aside for a moment, it's certainly not unheard of for a person with radical beliefs to undergo a sea change that results in the assumption of a diametrically opposed viewpoint. The ancient Greeks even had a word for it, first coined by Joannes Stobaeus in the fifth century: *enantiodromia*. This concept is also foreshadowed in the philosophy of Heraclitus, a Greek from the late sixth century BCE, who writes: "It is the opposite that is good for you."

In 1921 the psychologist Carl Jung theorized that *enantiodromia* is triggered by a mechanism in the unconscious that engenders a new equilibrium in consciousness. According to Jung, "when an extreme, one-sided tendency dominates conscious life, in time an equally powerful counterposition is built up," resulting in the "emergence of the unconscious opposite."[7] Jung was also drawing on Plato's aphorism in the *Phaedo*: "Everything arises in this way, opposites from their opposites."

But apart from the psychological dynamics that might be at work in such phenomena, this sort of vociferous political debate among "patriotic" right-wingers was not all that uncommon in the late 1960s. King is clearly an "old school" zealot: in his view, JFK veered too far to the left and needed to be removed to preserve the status quo business interests. But as a former soldier who fought against Hitler and Tojo on the battlefields of World War II, he has a problem with some of the neo-Fascist notions that are now being espoused by his murderous colleagues. King is also no fool, and he realizes that economic disparity sends

---

[7] See Carl Jung, *Psychological Types*, first published in German in 1921.

some men off to war to die in the rice paddies of Vietnam while others escape a military draft by lingering in expensive Ivy League colleges. In other words, King gets his hands dirty in supporting Establishment interests, but he does so without deluding himself: he knows how things really work. In addition, he's one of those right-wingers who don't necessarily buy into the Vietnam War jingoism or the need to emulate Hitlerian solutions of racial extermination (in this case, the liquidation of the Southeast Asian masses). He wonders: Isn't that the sort of thing that he and his generation fought against – and a cause that so many died for?

But Prince and Noslen are incapable of comprehending all this. To these neo-Fascists, the ends justify the means, no matter how vicious or inhuman. When this is revealed via a witty but bleak dialogue in the play's concluding scenes, the author sets the stage for a final twist of fate; and the thickheaded Prince feels he has no other choice but to usurp the assassins' throne.[8]

---

[8] Regarding this passage in the play, my colleague Al Rossi adds this insightful remark: "I am impressed particularly by the sophistication of Marks' characterization of the plotters as having different agendas. We should probably not forget the Brutus vs. Cassius paradigm here from *Julius Caesar* in this regard. Moreover, though not quite the same, it's also reminiscent of the uneasy alliance between neoliberals (the financier / corporatist / rentier class) and neoconservatives (the crazy military brinkmanship imperialists) that has had its ups and downs over the years but continues to function. To see this dynamic as having emerged from the alignment of interests that resulted in the assassination of JFK is definitely vatic, whether realized by Marks in an accord with dramatic or psychological principles of verisimilitude or not. There's also something of this in the screenplay of *Executive Action*, with differing viewpoints emerging from the characters played by Burt Lancaster, Robert Ryan, and Will Geer, but it certainly is not problematized in the same way in which Marks makes

Besides creating a drama that pivots upon King's *enantiodromian* reaction, Marks is also implying that the forces that killed Kennedy (at first, symbolized by King) eventually metastasized into even more demonic elements (personified by Prince and Noslen), leading to the imperialist policies of Nixon to Reagan to George W. Bush – a presidential rogue's gallery. And one that Marks not only witnessed firsthand, in real time, but that he continued to chronicle and critique until shortly before his death in 1999. He was one of the few who saw where all this was leading, and he tried to warn us through the vehicle of his self-published screeds – like a voice ringing out in the wilderness.

For example, one of the most percipient points raised in MMF-1 concerns what will happen in the aftermath of the Warren Commission. Marks boldly asserts that its lies will only serve to poison our collective national psyche:

> It can now be said that the American people do not believe anything stated in the "Report." Due to this lack of belief, a cynicism has now gathered among the Citizenry that bodes ill for the Nation. A Nation whose moral fiber has been torn and shattered cannot long live; for when the Nation's spirit is destroyed, no Nation will live [...]

As a result of this toxic brew of cynicism and despair, the nation's youth will grow disaffected, the American Dream will invert into nightmare, and a sense of hopelessness and a loss of vision will escalate throughout the decades and well into the future.

---

this a kind of linchpin for his dénouement." Al Rossi, private communication, December 26, 2022.

This is precisely what we, as a nation, have inherited today.

The same theme is explored in a final scene in the play, fittingly titled "Decay in the American Dream," when King tells Prince: "A nation without vision can never progress toward the future." In Marks' next assassination text, *Two Days of Infamy* (March 1969), he writes:

> Perhaps it was the cynicism, inherent in citizens of all nations, that convinced the American citizenry that the "Report" issued by the Warren Commission was supported by rotten timbers incapable of supporting the truth. The suspicion increased in the same ratio and in the same speed as smog increased with the density of automobiles on a Los Angeles freeway. The American people were becoming deeply convinced that the Commission had perpetrated a gigantic, gruesome hoax the like of which concealed a conspiracy that reached into the very gut of American government and society.

And in *Coup d'État!* (February 1970) he adds that the Commission's misdeeds led to the public's "erosion of faith" in governmental institutions.

In his play about the Sixties assassinations, *A Time to Die, A Time to Cry, or, Murders Most Foul!* (1979), Marks introduces a new character: Noslen's brother Ramal. In one scene Ramal remarks: "The country is out of kilter. Nobody trusts anyone. Something's cooking. I can't see what's in the pot." Reflecting on the JFK assassination, he inquires: "But was it worth it? Look at our country today. Faith has been destroyed in the governing process." To which Noslen concludes: "I guess this lack of trust started when the Warren Commission whitewashed the whole thing."

In that version of the play, Marks is unequivocal about who was the mastermind behind the assassination, when he has Ramal add: "[CIA Director] Dulles marked him for death when he resigned."

* * *

I have yet to come across a public notice or advertisement for Marks' first play in any of the media archives covering this period. Other than the fact that it was copyrighted on February 19, 1968 almost nothing is known about its genesis or history. It was only due to a search of his work in the Copyright Office that I was made aware of its existence. With the help of Marks' daughter, Roberta Marks, after filling out numerous forms and affidavits and responding to seemingly endless emails, on April 30, 2021 we finally managed to pry a copy of this eighty-one page manuscript from the labyrinthine Library of Congress.

Unlike Marks' subsequent plays, this particular version is never listed as a published work on any of his book jackets. But later versions of the drama were issued under his "Bureau of International Affairs" imprint, and they appear to have been substantially altered and expanded. For example, in 1970 he published a playscript with the title *A Time to Die, A Time to Cry* and described it as "A three-act play concerning the three murders that changed the course of history: President Kennedy, Martin Luther King, and Senator Robert F. Kennedy." And the 1979 version of *A Time to Die, A Time to Cry* is subtitled *Murders Most Foul!* (note the plural phrase: Murder<u>s</u>).

Although we don't know if this first playscript was ever given a public reading, one may infer that it was rehearsed or performed at least once. For, in his "Note to Producers and Directors," Marks writes: "Originally the actors had played the scene 'Who Speaks for God?' as Scene I of Act III. Some people liked it in that place; others were outspoken in saying that it belonged in the […] final scene of Act III."

I suspect that he refrained from publishing the manuscript because, less than two months after he registered it, Martin Luther King was assassinated, on April 4, 1968; and about two months later, on June 6, 1968 Robert Kennedy was also felled by assassins' bullets. With such historic events rapidly unfolding, Marks probably felt obliged to catch up with them. However, he may have been overwhelmed; for the first version is far more successful than the 1979 playscript, which I also obtained from the Copyright Office. The latter treatment attempts to go in so many different directions that it becomes bloated and is difficult to follow with any degree of enthusiasm.

Marks continued to rework his play all the way through 1988, when a final version was deposited in the Copyright Office: one that's since been reported as "lost." All the more reason to be thankful that this first version managed to survive, tucked away in one of the dusty cardboard boxes of our nation's disordered archives for fifty-three years.

– Rob Couteau

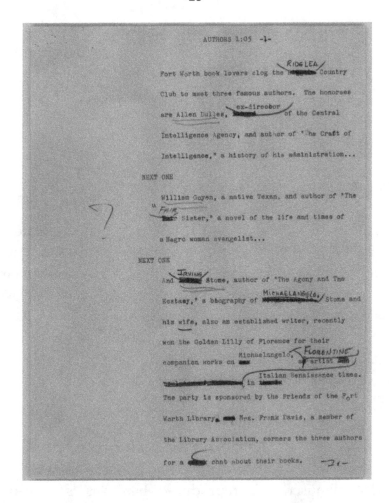

Less than a month before the assassination, on October 27, 1963, Allen Dulles visited Fort Worth, Texas, supposedly to promote his new book, *The Craft of Intelligence*. He was joined by two other authors, William Goyen and Irving Stone. In an unwitting nod to Dulles' perennial power behind the scenes, the reporters momentarily forgot that he was no longer (officially) in charge of the Agency: "Fort Worth book lovers clog the Ridglea Country Club to meet three famous authors. The honorees are Allen Dulles, ~~director~~ ex-director of the Central intelligence Agency …"

Source: "News Script from the WBAP-TV/NBC station in Fort Worth, Texas, covering a news story about authors Allen Dulles, William Goyen, and Irving Stone attending a meet-and-greet party at Fort Worth's Ridglea Country Club. October 27, 1963." KXAS-NBC 5 News Collection, UNT Libraries Special Collections, accessed at The Portal to Texas History.

Title Page of the Original Manuscript:

[Copyright stamp:] February 19, 1968.

[Copyright code number:] DU70838.

"A Murder Most Foul! Or, A Time to Die; A Time to Cry."

A three-act play that reveals how a chief of state was assassinated; who planned the assassination; how and why this most foul murder was committed on the 22nd day of November, in the year of Our Lord, 1963. The play that solves his assassination, by Stanley J. and Ethel M. Marks.

A note on the text:

Marks' manuscript is reproduced here "as is" except for minor corrections involving grammar and continuity, and several illustrations have been added.

For reasons that he explains later on, the names of various intel agencies are creatively altered. The Federal Bureau of Investigation is rendered as the "Internal Investigating Bureau," or IIB. The "EIA" is synonymous with the CIA, and the Secret Service is now the "SSB."

Preface by Stanley J. Marks

"A Murder Most Foul!" is an attempt to portray events prior, during, and after the murder of President John F. Kennedy on November 22, 1963.

"The Bay of Pigs" was the match that lit the flame of hatred that pulled the triggers, which sent four bullets smashing into the body of President John F. Kennedy. Bullets which not only snuffed out his life but also the soul and vision that represented the ideals of the United States of America.

The authors have relied solely upon the 888-page report issued by the Warren Commission; the words of testimony and exhibits published in the Commission's twenty-six volumes; the exhibits that are, or were, in the National Archives; and the interviews published in the various newspapers or statements made over electronic communications systems.

Every factual statement uttered by the actors relating to the murder can be read or seen by the reader in the above-enumerated sources.

Events, past or present, are always subject to interpretation. To interpret, one must have the truth.

The philosopher Spinoza once said: "He who would distinguish the true from the false must have an adequate idea of what is true and what is false. "

The testimony of witnesses, given under oath, has proved beyond a reasonable doubt that a conspiracy murdered President John F. Kennedy. The official reports of the Federal Bureau of Investigation, the United States Secret Service Bureau, and the Dallas Police Department have upheld the charge that a conspiracy, in fact and in law, murdered President John F. Kennedy.

The Commission, in an attempt to conceal these vital reports, refused to permit the publication these official government reports in either the "Report" or in the twenty-six volumes of the "Hearings."

The KEY to the solution to the question, "Did a conspiracy murder President John F. Kennedy?" can be found in the *New York Times* of November 22, 23, and 24, 1963; in the *Dallas Times-Herald* of November 22 and 23, 1963; and in volumes 2, 3, 6, 18, 19, 21, 24, and 26 of the "Hearings." The suppressed reports and photographs of the Federal Bureau of Investigation and the United States Secret Service can be read and seen in the National Archives.

"Of what value is a nation if it's people have no vision?"[9]

Note to the producer and director:

This play, "A Murder Most Foul!" deals with facts and not with a Freudian interpretation of the characters of the play as in *Hamlet* or *Macbeth*.

The play can thus deal only in fact and the characters are subordinate to the main theme of the play, which reveals the methods used to murder President John F. Kennedy; why he was murdered; and how his murder changed the course of history.

No attempt is made to understand the reasons why the Warren Commission issued a report based upon deceit, deception, and duplicity. As a matter of law it was the effort of two commissioners who proved that the Commission's alleged

---

[9] Marks is no doubt paraphrasing from Proverbs 29:18: "Where there is no vision, the people perish" (King James Version).

murderer could not and did not murder either President John F. Kennedy or the policeman. Ironically, it was evidence produced by the Commission itself that proved the existence of a conspiracy.

Thus, the play deals only with the preparation and consummation of the murder.

The cast is an all-male cast. Every actor is important, and if one breaks down, the entire play suffers. As this is a play concerning a conspiracy, the words of each actor, as in a conspiracy, is as important as those spoken by another actor.

The major speaking roles are those of King, Noslen, and Prince. These three appear in all the scenes in Act I and Act III. Upon their shoulders rest the framework of the play. In Act III, these three actors reveal the face not in the mirror, but in the conscience, of the United States of America.

The characters number thirteen, but it is entirely possible to cast this play with a minimum of eight male actors, as it is entirely possible for one actor to carry two rolls. The construction of the play permits this.

In Act I, Scene I, no actor is on stage.

In Act I, Scene II, only one actor, King, is seen, but he speaks no lines.

In Act I, Scene III three speaking actors, King, Noslen, and Prince, are the main characters. The actors, who simply act but speak not, are seen. These two silent actors should be used in Act II in speaking roles.

In Act II, Scene I, the actors are: Executor (pronounced as in "executioner"), Lion, Tiger, and Dancer, and two other Americans, Pilot and Marine.

In Act II, Scene II, the characters are: Executor, Lion, Tiger, and Dancer.

In Act II, Scene III, the actors are Executor, Lion, Bulldog, and Hawk.

In Act III, Scene I, the Battlefield Chaplain, and the Church Chaplain.

In Act III, Scene I and Scene III, King, Noslen, and Prince.

Thus, the total number of parts would be King, Noslen, Prince, Executor, Lion, Pilot, Marine, Tiger, Dancer, Bulldog, Hawk, Battlefield Chaplain, and Church Chaplain. Thirteen parts, but the structure of the play, as can be seen, permits a number of actors to portray two parts.

Act I, Scene I: "Prologue."

"A Murder Most Foul!" does not commence in the standard method of "Curtain going up!" The play commences in total darkness with only the "Exit" lights lit in accordance with fire laws.

As the fire curtain slowly rises (not the stage curtain), martial music is heard by the audience. Thus, selections should be well known military airs such as "The Stars and Stripes Forever," "American Patrol," "Washington Post March," "Caissons go Rolling Along," "Halls of Montezuma," "Wild Blue Yonder," and "Anchors Aweigh."

In the background of the song should be heard crowd noises and cheering.

Suddenly, in the middle of "Anchors Aweigh," shots from a military rifle ring out, a burst of three or four shots; and a woman's voice screams in anguish:

"My God, my God, they've killed him; they've killed him!"

Three more shots ring out; another woman's voice screams:

"Oh, my God, they're going to kill us all!"

Three more shots ring out, and a man's voice is heard:

"For God's sake, get out of here; get us out!"

The roar of the crowd increases, and the wail of a siren is heard and then fades into the distance.

As the siren fades away so does the noise of the crowd. As all sounds fade, the swelling music from the "Dead March From Saul" comes forth, then the wail of the bagpipes, interposed with the roll of drum beats, followed by the clippety-clop of horses' hooves on the pavement.

As this sound becomes muted, three volleys of gunfire are heard, and, during that gunfire, the roar of jet planes is heard. As the roar fades away, "Taps" is heard.

End of Act I, Scene I.

Note to the producer and director:

Actors who must appear to be Cuban are: Tiger, Dancer, Bulldog, and Hawk. The others are all citizens of the United States.

In Act II, Scene I, two false Oswalds are seen but not heard. There is more than sufficient evidence in the report and the hearings to prove that, in the conspiracy, a minimum of three Oswalds were used. Those two Oswald's are seen for less than two minutes, thus they can be used in regular speaking roles in the play. (A confident director need only use eight male actors for the production of "A Murder Most Foul!")

The use of a tape recorder in Act I, Scene I, and Act III is of the utmost importance. The recordings must come on perfect queue.

In Scene III of Act I, the voices of the police and the various radio announcers must come through the radio, which is on the secretary's desk. It must come through loud and clear. Background noises must be used to lend authenticity to the radio voice.

The rifle shots that are heard in Act I, Scene I and in Act III, Scene III must be actual rifle shots from a 7.65 rifle, and firecrackers must not be substituted for that sound.

As for stage props, the key element would be the use of a slide projector and a screen, which must be of sufficient height so that the entire audience can see the picture projected. Although easels are requested to be used in Act II, scene III there is no objection to the use of a slide projector.

It is not necessary to have elaborate sets for any scene of the play. It is not the cost of the stage setting that will make or break the play; only actors can do that.

The cartons actually carried by the two actors in Act II, Scene II must be weighted, and it is only in this scene where the two actors will actually raise a sweat!

The rifles must be authentic, and the actors using them must know how to "dry load," aim, and pull the trigger.

The final words spoken in the play are the identical words used to open the play.

This play, "A Murder Most Foul!" has been arranged in such a fashion that a producer or director has the freedom of choice in concluding the play by reversing the scenes in Act III.

If the director desires a shorter play within certain time limitations, then the third act should be revised to be played with only two scenes.

Act III, Scene I, would be the scene titled "The Critique," and Scene II of Act III would become the final scene; that is, the one called "Who Speaks for God?"

Originally the actors had played the scene "Who Speaks for God?" as Scene I of Act III. Some people liked it in that place; others were outspoken in saying that it belonged in the concluding scene, or as the final scene of Act III.

There is no loss of dramatic sense if "Who Speaks for God?" is played at the conclusion of either "The Critique" or "Decay in the American Dream." This "Who Speaks for God? scene should be played, as the authors believe that the questions must be answered by the American people. The wrong answers will eventually lead to World War III.

The value of the scene and titled "Decay in the American Dream" brings the American people face to face with the conditions that are, and that could become, a standard method of life.

The McCarran Act,[10] also known as the Concentration Camp Law, is not a myth. It is the law of the land. Federal detention warrants, issued under the code name Federal Dragnet, are not a myth. The federal agencies, which have the obligation to administer this Concentration Camp Law, have admitted before the Congressional hearings and to other persons who have questioned those agencies that the concentration camp sites have been selected and can be used immediately upon the declaration of insurrection by the president of the United States.[11]

---

[10] The Internal Security Act of 1950 (also known as the McCarran Act) required the Communist Party and twenty-four other organizations that were accused of being Communist to register with the Justice Department. Congress passed the McCarran Act despite the veto of President Harry Truman, who was concerned that it posed a serious threat to the First Amendment rights of freedom of speech. But here Stanley is specifically referring to the McCarran-Walter Act (The Immigration and Nationality Act of 1952), which "upheld the national origins quota system established by the Immigration Act of 1924, reinforcing this controversial system of immigrant selection." Office of the Historian, Foreign Service Institute United States Department of State, history.state.gov.

[11] Colloquially known as the "Concentration Camp Law," it was still in effect when Stanley authored his play: "In December 1952, Attorney General J. Howard McGrath designated six potential camp sites under the provisions of [the Emergency Detention Act, Title II of the Internal Security Act of 1950]. One of them was the Tule Lake site that had been formerly used to detain Japanese Americans. Ultimately, the law was never invoked and concentration camps were never activated ... [but] the law remained on the books for nearly twenty years [...] After extensive hearings and complex Congressional maneuvering, Congress passed the Repeal bill, now H.R.234, on September 14, 1971, by an overwhelming majority (356-49). H.R.234 not only repealed Title II but also prohibited 'the establishment of the emergency

The purchase of the computer and its primary use has been acknowledged by the agency involved. One former officer in charge of a concentration camp has admitted that the wives and children of the person arrested under the McCarran Act will [also] be taken to the camp.

The statements uttered by various political leaders to exterminate non-white nations are a matter of public record. The power of nuclear weapons as used in this play is not speculation but fact, uttered by various military officers appearing before the Congress of the United States.

In 1968, a presidential election year, this scene can easily be updated as the campaign rolls along.

In 1968 more than a presidential election is involved; it is our conscience.

---

detention camps.' President Richard M. Nixon signed it into a law on September 25, 1971. The Emergency Detention Act ended its twenty-one years of life without ever being invoked." See "Emergency Detention Act, Title II of the Internal Security Act of 1950," Encyclopedia.densho.org.

Act I, Scene II: "Rifles, Rifles, Everywhere."

PLACE: Dallas, Texas; November 18, 1963.

SET: As "Taps" comes to its mournful conclusion, the stage curtain is raised and the stage lights are set at half strength so that a mood of conspiracy is set.

The stage is set to portray an expensive looking executive office. A six-foot executive desk is placed at the left front area of the stage. Behind the desk is a leather chair as large as a judicial chair used in a courtroom.

Near the left wall, as seen by the audience, is a desk and chair for a secretary. On this desk is a yellow rose in a bud vase, which is placed near the right side of the desk. Near the center outer ledge is a small flag holder, which contains small Confederate and Texas state flags. On the wall behind the left side of the secretary's desk is the secretary's book table with one shelf. On the top of the table is a good-sized radio, which contains three bands: standard, police, shortwave.

In the first act, this radio plays an important role, in that from it will emanate the voices of the radio commentators and the police. It must be properly attached to the tape recorder behind the scenes so that it can play properly and on schedule. Slightly beyond is a bar.

In the left rear corner of the stage is a large Texas flag.

In the right rear corner of the set is a large Confederate flag.

Centered against the back wall is a fireplace with a mantel running slightly beyond, on both ends. On the mantelpiece, centered, is a large derrick, painted or glazed in gold. At the top of the derrick is a small Confederate flag.

There should be two doors, one on the left side of the stage, beyond and near the left of the bar. This door should open into the set so that the audience cannot see within it. Another door is placed on the right side of the stage, near the front and a little toward the rear, in line with the secretary's desk. This door also opens toward the audience.

Centered between the right door and the right corner is a large executive couch. In front of this couch is a coffee table, which is in proportion to the couch. Near this table are three executive chairs.

On the executive desk is a desk telephone, and on the left corner a flag holder containing a small flag of Texas and the Stars and Bars. In the front center is a desk set.

On the wall over the executive couch, above the heads of any of the actors who sit on the couch, are five rifles. These rifles are set in plastic clips in a horizontal manner. The bottom two rifles are the military type, and each of them has a telescopic sight. The rifle above it is a double-barrel shotgun. The two above it are 30-30 rifles.

On each wall are the heads of two different types of animals, for a total of six animal heads.

The floor, as one would expect, is fully carpeted, with the color to match the furniture.

All furniture should be on gold casters so that set changes can be made quickly.

A large-sized golden calf of mammon is placed in the front of the door at the couch's left side. The calf is sitting on its haunches, slightly turned toward the audience.

King enters from the door at right front stage and walks directly to the bar across the room. He goes behind the bar, takes out a whiskey decanter and shot glasses. Pours a shot into the glass, gulps sit down, shakes his head, then places glass and decanter on the top of the bar.

He walks over to the guns on the wall, removes the two rifles that have the telescopic sights, and lays both of them on the couch, making sure that they do not touch each other.

After laying down the rifles, King walks over to the left wall closet, opens it, and pulls out a large-sized golf bag. On the handle is a price tag, which dangles from the leather grip. He carries the bag over to the executive couch.

Leaning the golf bag against the couch so that it will not fall, King picks up one of the rifles and takes aim, in the exact fashion that any rifleman would, at each animal head. As he aims at each of these six heads, he pulls the trigger. Thus, he is conducting a "dry run," and he would be working the bolt of the rifle. He must cock and pull the trigger six times. After he finishes with that rifle, he repeats the identical performance with the other rifle. Be sure that King has placed the telescopic sight against his right eye as he pulls the trigger.

After he concludes his "dry run" with the first rifle, he lays it down on the couch, and after the second "dry run" both rifles are again on the couch. Now he picks up the golf bag. Then, as if suddenly remembering, he replaces the golf bag against the couch, walks to the closet, and takes out a brown blanket. Retracing his steps to the couch, he picks up one rifle, wipes off the entire rifle with the blanket, and puts that rifle into the golf bag. Taking the second rifle, he first wipes it off and then wraps the rifle in a blanket and puts that rifle into the golf bag.

After placing both rifles into the golf bag, King lays the bag on the couch and walks over to the executive desk. Taking a key from his pocket, King unlocks the last drawer on the right side of the desk and withdraws a small package. As he walks back toward the couch, the package falls from his hands and bullets spill out. As he stoops to pick them up, King reaches into his back pocket, takes out a handkerchief, and picks up the bullets, then replaces them in the box.

Reaching the couch, king inserts the box of bullets into the bag's golf ball pocket, first removing the white paper wadding from that pocket and stuffing it into one of his pockets. Closing the pocket, he rips off the price tag and stuffs that into his pocket.

King now wipes off the golf bag with his handkerchief and then carries the golf bag to the stage door right, making sure that he grips the bag with the handkerchief so as not to leave fingerprints. Then he opens the door and makes a motion to some unseen person.

The hands grab the bag from him. The audience cannot see anything but the hands.

After closing the door, King again turns to the bar, pours himself a drink, and replaces both the glass and decanter behind the bar. Then he walks to the door. As he flicks the light switch, the stage darkens and he walks out, closing the door behind him.

CURTAIN

End of Act I, Scene II.

Act I, Scene III: "The Death Watch."

TIME: November 22, 1963, 12:25 p.m. to 8:00 p.m.

PLACE: Dallas, Texas. An executive office.

SET: The same as in Act I, Scene II, with the exception that the two rifles with telescopic sights are missing.

CHARACTERS: NOSLEN, PRINCE, TWO NON-SPEAKING ACTORS, KING.

CURTAIN

(As the curtain goes up, four men are on the stage. One man is sitting on the couch, nursing a drink. Another man is at the bar, pouring out a drink. NOSLEN and PRINCE are sitting on the executive chairs at the coffee table conversing in low, inaudible voices. All the men are dressed in business suits except NOSLEN, who is dressed in Western style, wearing cowboy [boots], but his pant legs are not tucked inside his boots. The NONSPEAKING ACTORS wear glasses, one with horned rims; the other, the old-fashioned rimless.

The man at the bar, with drink in hand, walks over to the gun rack, looks, and taps the sitting man on the couch, who looks up and sees the man gesture at the gun rack, pointing to the two empty spaces. The sitting man shrugs his shoulders, and the other man then sits down beside him.

NOSLEN rises, and as he does so the telephone of the executive desk rings. He walks to the desk and picks up the phone. He listens for about ten seconds and hangs up the phone. Now he walks over to the bar, pours a drink for himself, and strides toward the fireplace.

As he reaches it, he raises his glass in a salute, first to the Texas flag, then to the Confederate flag. As he dashes his glass into the fireplace, he says:)

"We got the son of a bitch! We got him!"

(The three other actors, who followed him as he strode toward the fireplace, now each salute the two flags in the same manner and also throw their glasses in the fireplace. After the glasses have been thrown, NOSLEN and PRINCE walk back to the executive desk; the other two reseat themselves. After seating themselves:)

PRINCE: Now, what?

NOSLEN: We wait.

PRINCE: Wait for what?

NOSLEN: We wait for him. Now, shut up!

(A slight wait. Then the door at the right stage front opens. In walks KING. As he walks toward the executive desk, all actors rise.)

KING: (Still standing behind his desk, asks NOSLEN:)

KING: Well, have you heard the results?

NOSLEN: Yes, sir. The first report came in a few minutes ago. He is as good as dead. We made four hits; two in the head, one in the throat slightly below the neck tie knot, and one in the back.

KING: Good shooting! But what about the others?

NOSLEN: Unfortunately the governor was hit twice, perhaps three times. How serious, our man did not know. The women escaped.

KING: Well, no one is perfect even with telescopic sights. Turn on the radio.

(NOSLEN walks over to the radio behind the secretary's desk and turns it on. Be sure to have it sound natural, so the first words will have to be in the middle of a sentence:)

ANNOUNCER: "... broken out. I am trying to get near the hospital entrance. Police Ser.. Hey! Get off my wires! Sergeant, sergeant! Is he dead; is he dead? Are they ...

SECOND RADIO VOICE: Stan, Stan, I'm taking over. Everyone is milling around the plaza. Police are all over the area. Wait! Police have just come out of the warehouse building. They have a man with them who is carrying a rifle. The crowd is now surging around them; more police are converging on the crowd, trying to protect him. Now they have shoved the prisoner into a police squad car. I do not know the meaning of this. Wait. Hold on!

(Silence for about five seconds.)

What's that? Stan, I have been informed that the sheriff's police have also arrested a man carrying a rifle. This man was captured near the grassy hill by the fence. What did you say? (Silence.) Oh, Stan, a passerby said that this man was seen by two or three witnesses as the rifleman. He was taken to the sheriff's jailhouse. Now I see several policemen running into a building and ...

FIRST ANNOUNCER: Bill, I have to cut in. A priest has just entered the hospital. It looks serious. I think that we should ex ...

THIRD RADIO VOICE. This is the Ace Broadcasting System. This is a special bulletin. The chief of state is dead. He died from the result of bullet wounds in the head. Two men have been apprehended by various police authorities who have thus far refused to release any information. We now return you to Dallas, Texas.

FIRST ANNOUNCER: A hospital physician, who was one of the six striving to save the life of the chief of state, has officially announced his death. The physician stated that death was due to the result of a massive wound over the left temple. He also said ... (sobs) I can't ... I can't ...

KING: Turn it off!

(NOSLEN turns off radio. KING now rises from his chair and moves toward the bar. NOSLEN, anticipating him, goes to the bar and pours out a drink. He gives it to KING, who strides toward the fireplace. He salutes the Texas flag, then the Confederate flag, gulps down the drink, and hurls the glass into the fireplace. As the glass shatters, ALL ACTORS arise and applaud. KING bows to all of them, who return his bow, and KING returns to his judicial chair.)

KING: Let us keep up with the news. Please turn it on again.

(NOSLEN does so.)

THIRD RADIO VOICE: ... announcement that the chief of state has been murdered has shocked and outraged the capital. We have been informed that a red alert has been given to all our armed forces, here and overseas. Several members of both chambers have urged the nation to issue a declaration of war against the Bearded One and an immediate invasion of that island. A few others have urged an immediate break in relations with Moscow.

No one here knows who the murderers are, as the Dallas Police have clamped on a tight security.

We have also been informed that neither the chief nor the assistant chief of the SSB accompanied the chief of state to Dallas. The former head of the SSB has stated that this is unprecedented, since it has been a custom that one or the other accompany the chief of state whenever he leaves the capital.

Whether a coup d'état has been attempted or is being attempted is not known, but the fact that both the secretary of defense and the secretary of state are not in the country lends some credence to that fact.

We have also received word that, in addition to the two men arrested near the scene of the crime, another man, who was five or six miles from the scene, was arrested for the killing of a city policeman. What connection this man has with the murder of the ...

KING: Shut it off. (NOSLEN turns off radio.) Well, gentleman, we may or may not get our war with the Bearded One. We may, if the cards fall right, be able to implicate the Moscow Reds, and either have a complete break in relations with them or have our war with them also. But whatever does happen, I can assure you that we, our group, now control the government. Within the next seven or eight months, people, our kind of people, will be sitting in the chairs of power. An entire new philosophy of government will slowly emerge.[12] So, let us all have patience. We have waited three years; we can wait a little longer.

NOSLEN. Now what do we do?

KING: I want you and Prince to remain here. The others can leave. I will see all of you tomorrow night at our social.

(The other two actors rise, go to KING, and shake his hand. Then they leave by the right front stage door. As the door closes, all three, KING, NOSLEN, and PRINCE, go to the bar and each fills his glass.)

KING: Let us sit at the table and relax. This drink should do it.

(ALL THREE MEN now sit at the coffee table, facing the audience but in a semicircle, so that each can talk to the other in a normal fashion.)

PRINCE: Well, it's finished.

KING: Finished? Hell, it's just begun.

PRINCE: I don't understand. I don't understand.

---

[12] Cf. Jack Ruby's jail cell statement to Chief Justice Warren: "A whole new form of government is going to take over the country, and I won't live to see you another time."

KING: (Mimicking.) I don't understand. I don't understand.

NOSLEN: From a historical background, Mr. King, what is happening?

KING: What we are witnessing is the transfer of power by the use of an invisible coup d'état!

PRINCE: A coup d'état? Now, that I do not understand.

KING: What everyone is witnessing, but not understanding, is a perfect transfer of power through the use of a democratic constitution. Illegal in the manner by which a chief of state was removed by murder; legal by the assumption of power by the vice-chief of state. He assumed power honestly and legitimately. What is more natural than when the murdered victim's place is assumed by the second choice of the victim's own political party? Remember that both the victim and his successor were legally elected and properly installed. What our countrymen and the rest of the world is waiting to hear is the answer to the question: "who murdered him and why?"

NOSLEN: Will anyone, outside of our group, ever come up with the answer?

KING: Oh, yes, eventually. We may be able to keep the reasons why the chief was murdered from our generation. However, sometime in the future, students of the event will finally discover the fact that he was done away with because our group believed that the chief's conduct of our national and international affairs was inimical to both us and the nation. Another man said it in another manner: What was good for GM was good for the nation. Just as he placed his interests first, so do we.

You see, Prince, the reason you failed to understand what is happening today is that you believe what you read and hear, but you are too damn stupid, or lazy, to do your own thinking.

PRINCE: I resent that! I had three years of history in college, and I think I know history.

KING: I doubt if you know the history of your own life. You know nothing of history. Just look at the history taught in our schools today. It's not worth a tinker's damn. According to our history books our country grew into a world power because the wands of God touched only the white Anglo-Saxon Protestant. In fact, after reading one of those alleged history books, one would receive the impression that the WASPs were the ones who guided God and gave to him their wisdom, which he has accepted.

NOSLEN: Oh, come now, Mr. King, that is an extreme example.

KING: Is it? Show me a history book now being used in the high schools and colleges that is partial to the minority groups in our country. Who in the hell do you think made this country? The direct and only descendants from the Mayflower?

PRINCE: I had two of my kids go through public grammar and high school. Both of them are now in college, and I'll say this for them, they certainly know the names and dates that made our country great.

KING: For Christ's sake, Prince, grow up! That is all the schools teach, names and dates. But do the schools teach the reason why those names and dates are important? Hell, no! How the hell can teachers teach if they have to act as babysitters six hours a day? Look at the number of college students who say that we do not need a Bill of Rights. How many times have I heard you say that the Fifth Amendment should be abolished?

PRINCE: Goddamn it! Yes, I say the Fifth should be abolished. Too damn many communists, gangsters, crooks, kooks, and hippies take the Fifth. That is what is destroying our nation. That damn Fifth!

KING: Prince, are you and I talking about the same Fifth? Are you talking about a bottle or the Constitution?

PRINCE: Don't get sarcastic with me, Mr. King. I'm not interested in the reasons behind the Fifth. I only know that certain people in this country are against everything I and my friends – good, solid, substantial Americans – stand for. If those people don't like it, we ought to send them back to where they came from.

KING: Where? To their mother's womb? You say, Prince, that you are against the Bill of Rights, or the first ten Amendments. Should we revoke the right to habeas corpus? What about freedom of religion? Or the press? Or the right to petition Congress? Or the use of torture to extract confessions? Or better yet, Prince, what would you do if the federal government took over your twenty-room mansion for quartering troops? Why, damn me, Prince, I thought you were a patriot; here I find you letting our brave soldier boys bed down in the rain, sleet, and snow. By God, Prince, you are acting like a damn subversive. Noslen, call the IIB, immediately, at once; we have a Red in our bosom!

NOSLEN: All right, all right. Let us get back to more serious business. (Laughing.)

KING: You are right. Turn on the radio. (NOSLEN goes over to radio and turns it on.)

SECOND RADIO VOICE: … has been arrested and taken to the jailhouse. All the personnel from the various news media are crowded into this small corridor outside the captain's office, and confusion still rains. Here's a police sergeant. Sergeant, sergeant! Who do you have in there?

SERGEANT'S VOICE: "If you'll all keep quiet, I will give you a statement. (Background noise dies down.) The Dallas Police captured a man in a theater some five miles away from the shooting. We believe that he is the man who shot the police officer between 1:06 and 1:10 p.m. this afternoon. We are continuing our questioning.

SECOND RADIO VOICE: Did you ask him if he had murdered the chief?

SERGEANT'S VOICE: I said he denied killing anyone.

SECOND RADIO VOICE: What about the two men captured near the hill, the one with the rifle?

SERGEANT'S VOICE: (Heatedly.) What the hell are you talking about?

SECOND RADIO VOICE: Why, the man captured by the deputy sheriff with a rifle in his hands.

SERGEANT'S VOICE: I know nothing about that man. Ask the sheriff.

SECOND RADIO VOICE: Then what about the other man?

SERGEANTS VOICE: What other man?

SECOND RADIO VOICE: For God's sake, what's going on here? The rifleman you cops captured in the building across the street from the depository. It was on the police radio broadcast.

SERGEANT'S VOICE: I don't know nothing. I'm only talking about the man we got in there. I'm only talking about that P. Patsy.

SECOND RADIO VOICE: P. Patsy? Who is he?

SERGEANT'S VOICE: The man we got in the captain's office. We're checking his prints to see if he has a record. As soon as we know, we will furnish you with the ...

FIRST RADIO VOICE: This is the ABS Dallas News Center reporting. We have interrupted the police conference to bring you up to date.

It is now known that a minimum of three men are in custody. The police have released the name of only one man, P. Patsy. This man was captured in a theater and is said to be involved in the murder of a Dallas policeman.

Why Patsy is being held or investigated for the murder of the chief of state is a mystery, for the only two eyewitnesses to the policeman's murder have given a description of the killer that does not resemble Patsy in the slightest degree.

Furthermore, the police have stated that shells from both a pistol and a revolver were were found, and Patsy's gun does not discharge an automatic shell.

From the spectators at the scene of the chief's murder, it is now known that a minimum of seven shots were fired at him. According to the hospital physicians, three bullets struck the governor, and one bullet was found on the ground.

From the location of the wounds in both the chief and the governor, plus the bullets that missed, it can only be interpreted that a minimum of two riflemen, perhaps three, were involved. This means that a ring of conspira ...

KING: Turn it off! (NOSLEN turns off radio.)

PRINCE: What the hell! Our plan did not include the murder of a cop!

NOSLEN: That's right, Mr. King. Patsy was not to be seen from 1:00 p.m. until he was captured in the theater.

KING: Don't panic! Patsy did not murder anyone. He was picked up as arranged and taken to the theater. He was supposed to draw attention to himself and he did. He perfected his part beautifully.

PRINCE: Then why was the cop killed?

KING: How in the hell do I know? Noslen, turn on the radio band and let us hear what they have to say. (NOSLEN turns on radio.)

POLICE VOICE: ... jacket. According to the only two eyewitnesses to the murder of our fellow police officer, the killer has bushy hair, is about five-foot-nine in height, has a very dark complexion, and weighs about 165 pounds. This murder was committed at 1:06 p.m., and this time has been substantiated by another witness who came upon the murder scene at 1:10 p.m. This killer is dangerous and should be approached with …

KING: Turn it off, Noslen. (NOSLEN does so.) Now, Prince, does that match Patsy's description?

PRINCE: No, I agree with you; but there is an element of danger involved.

KING: (In surprise.) An element of danger? What danger? The cop was killed at 1:06 p.m. and the police have the landlady's evidence that she saw him at a bus stop at 1:04. Do you believe that Patsy could run nine-tenths of a mile in two minutes flat? Why, that would be a world's track record.

PRINCE: Then why was Patsy arrested?

KING: Jesus Christ Almighty! Save us from horses' asses like you! Patsy was supposed to be arrested. He was. He was supposed to be arrested for the murder of the chief. He will be. The cops were supposed to find a rifle. They will. So they book him for the murder of the cop. So what? You idiot! I would not be surprised if another horse's ass in the DA's office will not try to charge the Bearded One and the Moscow Reds with the murders. If that occurs, we may have the war we want before he is even buried. You heard the red-alert report. Wake up!

NOSLEN: Stop being a worrywart, Prince. Everything will go A-OK. Mr. King, what have we accomplished today?

KING: We have changed the course of world history. You cannot see it now, but two or three years from today you will look back and have the satisfaction of knowing you helped change that course. Our group has eliminated a man whom we felt was directing this nation on paths inimical to our nation's interests.

PRINCE: But what about the new chief?

NOLEN: Have you forgotten that the new chief of state has grown up with us? He has broken bread with us; he believes in many of our ideas. Although he has no knowledge, today, of what his friends have done, he is in our background; we are in his. He may not realize it, but by a process of osmosis we have seeped into him.

PRINCE: But what can he do now?

KING: Now? Nothing. He must first consolidate his right to the highest office in this nation by being elected in '64. Once he obtains that right, he then becomes the most powerful man in the world. He is the only man alive who can press the nuclear button without consulting anyone. So, to obtain that position, he will religiously follow the path trod upon by the dead one. He will promise everything to everyone. His vocal commitment is not a legal one. We are in his background, and that will compel him to be one of us.

PRINCE: But that is nearly a year away. Hell, he may not be elected.

KING: You know, Prince, the way you talk leads me to believe I am libeling the horse. The new chief of state will wrap himself with the mantle worn by the dead one. The public will do the rest. So, Prince, what is a year for a lifetime of power?

NOSLEN: Philosophy, philosophy. How goes our plan?

KING: Turn on the radio and find out. (NOSLEN does so.)

SECOND RADIO VOICE: ... And can a man on the street give a description of the man at the sixth-floor window, captain?

CAPTAIN: No. Some officer said "We think the man who did the shooting at the window is a tall, white man"; that is all I have. This doesn't mean a thing, you know, because you can't tell five or six floors up whether a man is tall or short.

SECOND RADIO VOICE: Thank you, captain. Oh, inspector, inspector! You were in the automobile leading the chief's automobile. Did you see anything at the sixth-floor window when you heard the shots?

INSPECTOR: No. I do not remember seeing any object or anything like that such as a rifle or anything pointed out of the windows; there was no activity, no one moving around.

SECOND RADIO VOICE: Say, here before our microphone is one of the Dallas IIB agents. Could you tell us, sir, anything concerning that rifle found on the sixth floor?

AGENT'S VOICE: I cannot give you too much information. However, the rifle sent to us by the Dallas Police gives forth white smoke whenever it is discharged. The man who said he saw the man at the sixth-floor window denied he ever saw white smoke. Furthermore, in an affidavit to us he also said he could not identify anyone. So, no police agency of any kind has any witness.

SECOND RADIO VOICE: Sir, what about fingerprints?

AGENT'S VOICE: No. No fingerprints, although the rifle given to us by the Dallas Police was received in a well-oiled condition, and this in spite of the fact that the rifle was handled by several Dallas policemen.

SECOND RADIO VOICE: What does that mean?

AGENT'S VOICE. (Laughing.) Don't put me on the spot. Make your own guess.

KING: Noslen, turn it off. (As Noslen goes over to the radio:) No, wait a minute. Tune in London on the shortwave band. Let's hear what they are saying about the murder. (NOSLEN switches radio to shortwave band. Be sure and have some atmospheric sounds to lend authenticity.)

ENGLISH ANNOUNCER: ... And what is occurring in the city of Dallas tonight is a fascinating study in outrageous confusion. It is now approximately 7:00 p.m. in that city, and we have received a rather lengthy summary from out commentator who was traveling with the murdered chief of state.

The new chief of state has been sworn into the office and has reached his capital.

Within twenty minutes after the shots were fired the police agencies arrested a minimum of three men. Unconfirmed rumors have said a minimum of eight. However, two of the three men were arrested carrying rifles, and both of them were in the area of the murder site. These men are being held incommunicado.

Approximately 2:20 p.m., the police brought into the Dallas jail a man named P. Patsy who had been arrested for the murder of a policeman shot down some five miles from the area where the chief of state was murdered.

The police arrest sheet revealed the strange fact that Mr. Patsy was not only charged with the murder of the policeman, but also with the murder of the chief of state and the wounding of the governor. At 5:30 p.m., over a national radio and television broadcast, a high police official stated that they had absolutely no witnesses who could identify the murder of the chief of state. Therefore, how could Mr. Patsy be charged with the murder of the chief of state when he was brought into the police station?

Our communicator from the States has informed us that seven police officers and deputy sheriffs have identified the rifle found on the sixth floor of the depository building as a 7.65 German Mauser. Their statements have been confirmed by the district attorney of Dallas, who has had experience in the identification of firearms, as he was a former agent of the IIB. Thus there can be no doubt that the rifle found on the sixth floor was a German Mauser.

A Dallas newspaper in its final edition has stated, from its investigation, that the shots were not fired from the depository where the rifle was found but from the "extension of Elm Street, from just beyond the depository building at the corner of Elm and Houston Street." Our communicator checked that area and he reported that the name of the building is the Dal-Tex Building.

If this is so, and based on the newspaper report, then the Dallas Police have confused the name of the building. This seems to be correct, since the police radio broadcasts announced the arrest of one of the riflemen inside the Dal-Tex Building.

A preliminary report by both federal agencies – the IIB and the SSB – confirm the Dal-Tex Building as one of the ambushed sites, since the angle of fire, or the path of the bullet which struck the chief of state from the rear, has a forty-five to sixty-degree angle. The governor was struck from the front at a twenty-seven-degree angle of fire. This can only mean that the chief of state was struck and murdered in a classic crossfire ambush and that at least three men took part. Both agencies have issued statements that the chief of state was struck by two bullets and the governor by another one. This is a minimum of three bullets fired from different and separate ambush areas.

It has been disclosed by the Miami Florida Police Department that they forwarded, to both the IIB and the SSB, back in September 1963, tapes of a recording they had made of a confession by a man who was involved in various criminal acts. These acts were made in violation of law known in the States as the Civil Rights Act. The crimes ranged from arson of black homes and buildings to bombings, whippings, torture, and murder. In this man's confession he informed the Miami Police that an attempt would be made upon the chief's life when he would visit Dallas; and not only did he give the police the warning but he announced the fact the chief would be murdered from ambush and the buildings would be used as a site.

Both agencies have acknowledged the receipt of the tapes, but they have refused to divulge the contents.

Throughout the day of turmoil in Dallas, we have been receiving information that is staggering to contemplate. For not only did both bureaus received the tapes, but the SSB had only two of their agents guard the chief of state during his sleep on the night previous to the murder. There seems to have been no follow-up by either the SSB or IIB in ordering additional protection for the chief of state. This in spite of the fact that a

Dallas newspaper published an advertisement on the day of the murder calling for the implied death of a traitor who was none other than the chief of state.

Our commentator has also received information that, within one hour of the murder, a rumor swept the city of Dallas that a highly placed official of a Texas oil firm was airlifted out of the city under an assumed name. The airline has refused to confirm or deny that agents of the IIB were involved.[13]

Finally, as our time is running short, a Dallas newspaper has published a statement by a high official of the Dallas Police Department that has the implication that persons in either the Dallas administration or Dallas Police Department are involved in the murder.

An official of the Dallas Police stated "they had to bring him through town, and an agent told me they didn't want that either." The intriguing question is, thus, who are "they"? Why did the Dallas Police, against their own fears, bring the chief of state through the town? Why did the SSB have no desire to permit the chief of state to travel in an open automobile in the city of Dallas in an area surrounded by tall buildings? In view of the information on the Miami, Florida, police tapes, why did both the IIB and the SSB permit that parade? Did the SSB refuse to inform the chief that he was in danger, or did they inform the chief and then challenge his manhood? Why was the bubble[14]

---

[13] A reference to rumors that immediately after the assassination oil mogul H. L. Hunt was escorted by FBI agents to a plane flying him to Mexico, where he supposedly went into hiding. Hunt was known for his extremist views and his funding of various right-wing causes. JFK's proposal to remove the oil depletion allowance (the largest tax loophole in American history) would have negatively impacted upon Hunt's oil empire.

[14] In 1961 the White House leased a brand-new Ford Lincoln Continental limousine, whose sleek design also featured a clear

not used to protect the chief in a city that was noted for its hatred of the chief of state? The city that had tried to murder Ambassador Stevenson in September of this year.[15] Why does the official map of the cavalcade, published in yesterday's Dallas newspaper, show no double detour; and yet, in violation of all SSB rules and regulations, some Dallas Police official permitted the chief's automobile to not only make that dangerous double detour but also come to a complete halt on Houston and Elm Streets. Why?

One last word before we sign off for the night. Our communicator has filed his final bulletin which states that there was a fight between two SSB agents and another man carrying a revolver outside the operating room while the physicians were fighting to save the life of the chief of state. Three other men, with revolvers, also attempted to enter the same room. Why? No American newspaper has printed this story. So, the plot thickens. Until tomorrow at 6:00 a.m., this is the BBS, London, England. (Big Ben chimes twelve.)[16]

---

plastic "bubble top" roof. Few were aware that the removable plastic-topped covering was neither bulletproof nor bullet resistant.

[15] On October 24, 1963 U.N. Ambassador Adlai Stevenson gave a speech in Dallas on United Nations Day. Afterward, a "hostile crowd of about one hundred protesters surrounded the ambassador outside the auditorium. Many carried signs denouncing the U.N. – signs that had been stored at [Major General Edwin] Walker's home. Stevenson tried to reason with the protesters. Suddenly, one woman conked him on the head with her sign. A man spat on him. After police broke through the crowd to rescue him, Stevenson was heard to say, 'Are these human beings or are these animals?'" See Scott Parks, "Extremists in Dallas created volatile atmosphere before JFK's 1963 visit," *Dallas Morning News*, October 12, 2013.

[16] "Big Ben chimes twelve": A keynote signature of the British Broadcasting Corporation (BBC).

KING: That limey son of a bitch! That son of a bitch! (KING pounds desk.

PRINCE: What's wrong? What's wrong? Anything serious?

KING: No. Nothing I cannot handle. But that bastard was close. It's lucky it was an overseas broadcast (Phone rings.)

NOSLEN: (Picks up phone and listens for a moment.) Yes? Looks at KING.) Patsy is asking for a lawyer. Someone in New York.

KING: What code name did the caller use?

NOSLEN: "History." (King takes phone from NOSLEN.)

KING: History here. Yes, he told me. How does he look? Will he crack? You think so? All right, all right, your word is sufficient. You know how to handle his phone call to New York. No, Patsy was instructed to ask for that lawyer. Other lawyers? No, absolutely not! Hold on for a minute, I want to think. (King cradles phone in his lap as he talks to NOSLEN and PRINCE:)

It looks like Patsy's going to break. He may hold off for a day or two at the most. If the press get to him ... he'll have to go. Agreed? (Both NOSLEN and PRINCE nod their heads "yes.")

KING: (Speaking into phone.) Rattler, I want you to contact Stripper.[17] For safety's sake; also Hands and Doc. They will

---

[17] The "Stripper" character is based upon Dallas nightclub owner Jack Ruby, the mobbed-up proprietor of the Carousel Club: a "strip joint" patronized by both the underworld and the Dallas Police.

know what to do. When? Well, the cops will have to transfer him to another jail. That would be the best time. The press? Of course this is still a free country, and what would we do without it? The greater the number, the greater the confusion, and the easier the execution. Am I satisfied? Absolutely! Everyone is doing their work A-OK. Goodbye. (Hangs up phone. NOSLEN and PRINCE go back to coffee table; KING remains at desk.)

KING: You know, when I organized this event, I never thought the ramifications would be so great.

PRINCE: What do you mean?

KING: I found that a conspiracy is like throwing a stone in the water. From the center, the ripples keep getting larger and larger until it seems that the whole body of water is agitated. Everything those ripples touch reacts in a different manner. We murdered one man today, but a thousand, no, hundreds of thousands are going to die. No one on this earth will ever be the same.

NOSLEN: Well, if we control the events we control the world.

KING: No, Noslen, no one, but no one, controls anyone who has no desire to be controlled. A dictator is generally supreme because the people to whom he wants to dictate to accept that dictation. If a man gives up the fight to remain free, then he accepts the role of a slave. Under Hitler, the Germans wanted to be slaves and they became slaves.

NOSLEN: I feel no qualms. I still believe that what we did was for the betterment of my country. I'll let history be the judge. Perhaps some seventy-five years from today another

Shakespeare will write about the Julius Caesars and Mark Antonys of 1963. But I will not be here. So, why worry?

KING: You missed the point, Noslen. We have not only killed a man but we may also have killed the spirit of this nation.

Prince: Mr. King, I think that now that the deed has been successful we are entitled to know how this all happened.

KING: Yes, I agree. It is your neck as well as mine. So, let us go out and have our dinner. Then I will tell you how it all happened.

(ALL RISE and go out the right front stage door.)

CURTAIN

End of Act I, Scene III.

Act II, Scene I: "The Preparations."

TIME: October 1963

PLACE: An apartment in New Orleans.

STAGE: The dining room is an old-fashioned apartment in the home of a Cuban refugee.

Furniture consists of one dining room table, extended to seat six. Two dining room armchairs, four straight chairs from a set of six. Armchair at end of table, which is placed horizontal to stage.

On dining room table is a bottle of whiskey and six glasses. Ice in dish. A bowl or real fruit is also on table.

On left side of stage is a couch, beyond that is a TV set on wheels. Pictures on wall, etc. Floor lamps. Be sure that an electrical outlet is near the lower baseboard on the left, as it must be used for the slide projector. The furniture is not rich, but lower-middle Cuban style.

The rear of the stage must have windows which represent the street side of the house, and on the windows are drapes which close when pulled, as will be necessary when the slide projector is in use. On the right side of the wall, near the windows, should be a silver screen which is used for pictures from the slide projector. At right rear wall, like any apartment house, is a door which will be used as the entrance and exit.

Actors: TIGER, DANCER, LION, EXECUTOR (pronounced as in "executioner"), MARINE, and PILOT. The two CUBANS are dressed in Cuban sports clothes. PILOT in aviation uniform; MARINE in GI pants and sports shirt.

CURTAIN

(The two CUBANS are standing, smoking long panatela cigars. Lion is standing near the windows, looking out. Finally, TIGER and DANCER both sit down at the horizontal side of the table, facing the audience. As LION walks toward them, TIGER pours himself a drink and then offers bottle to DANCER, who does the same. As LION reaches the table, DANCER offers bottle to LION, who shakes head "no." LION sits down in armchair at right side of table.)

TIGER: What the hell's keeping them? Always we wait, wait.

LION: Relax, Tiger, relax. They'll soon be here.

Dancer: "Relax," he says! For nearly two years your friend says "Relax, relax, the time will come." And then what? Talk, talk, talk!

Lion: Patience, my hot-tempered Cuban, patience.

(Footsteps are now heard, and the door at the right rear stage opens. In walks EXECUTOR, in sports jacket, slacks, and ascot; followed by MARINE, wearing GI trousers, short-sleeve shirt opened at collar; and then PILOT, in airline uniform but with no insignia, with sleeves carrying four stripes denoting him as a captain.[18]

---

[18] "Pilot" is clearly based upon the assassination plotter, David Ferrie.

As EXECUTOR enters, the actors at the table rise. EXECUTOR goes to the armchair at the left side of the table, MARINE and PILOT sit to the CUBANS' left.

All actors may smoke, drink, or eat during this scene.

Lion: Welcome, Mr. Executor. We have been a little on edge.

TIGER: Yes, sir. This waiting is worse than the goddamn army. Every time I ask "When?" I get the same damn answer: "*Mañana.*"

EXECUTOR: The waiting is over. This is why we meet here today. Thank you, Tiger, for the use of your home. We will be here for some time but, when we finish, each of us will know what to do.

LION: Sir, has the day been selected?

EXECUTOR: Yes, the twenty-second of next month!

TIGER and DANCER reach across to shake EXECUTOR's hand, then they in turn shake hands with each other. TIGER then pours out a drink for each one and passes the glass to each one.

After each actor has a drink in their hand, they all stand and TIGER says:

Tiger: *Salud*! (They all drink, then all sit down.)

EXECUTOR: You all know that we are meeting here today because the Miami plan had to be canceled, because someone talked to the police.

DANCER: Talked? What was he, crazy?

EXECUTOR: No, yellow! The informer went to the Miami cops, and the chief of state was flown into Miami by helicopter. Naturally, I was informed immediately of both the confession and the change of plans, so I canceled the strike.

DANCER: Who talked?

EXECUTOR: Whoever he was, he is not in this world anymore. (All laugh, and the two Cubans applaud.)

LION: Was any vital information given to the cops?

EXECUTOR: None according to our plans, since the informer never knew if we were to hit him from Fort Worth or Dallas, just that the same outfit was going to kill him from ambush in one of those two cities. He did give them information regarding the leaders behind the outfits terrorizing the Civil Rights Movement.

LION: What about our department vis-à-vis the IIB and the SSB?

EXECUTOR: The police used a tape recorder on the informer and sent the original and a copy to both bureaus. What they are going to do I have no knowledge of at present; but since the stool pigeon never mentioned us, I am not worried. Marine (looking at MARINE), what do you think?

MARINE: The IIB won't do a damn thing. In my dealings with them I found that many of the agents think the same way we do. From conversations with my contacts, I gather a good number of them, like the heads of the Bureau, hate the chief and his entire family. They won't go into mourning when he's dead.

TIGER: Will there be any change in the overall plan?

EXECUTOR: One or two minor changes will be added or subtracted, but the overall scheme remains the same. We will discuss and decide where to use our riflemen today, and after today no changes.

TIGER: Will we have enough time to practice?

EXECUTOR: Definitely. Today is October third, and we have until the twentieth of next month to practice and iron out all the details. Let's see, that gives us about seven weeks. Yes, plenty of time.

LION: How many men will it take?

EXECUTOR: Just enough to do the job properly. We know that the chief will visit Dallas on both the twenty-first and twenty-second. We do not have his exact route, but we can deduce it from our previous knowledge as to how the Dallas police and the SSB will manage the parade. So, before we leave today, all of us will make the final decision.

Dancer: Then the plan is still the same? We hit him from the front and back?

EXECUTOR: Yes, from the front and back.

DANCER: That is good! Very good! Revenge is sweet!

Tiger: Yes, it is good. After that speech he gave at the Miami stadium, everyone believed him. That was nearly three years ago. Last year, when he had the Reds on the spot on the spot, he let them wiggle out of it. He should have used the bomb! He should have used it!

LION: Let's not cry over spilt milk. He will be dead by the night of the twenty-second. So let us make damn sure that nothing can go wrong.

EXECUTOR: (Slapping hand on table several times.) Now, listen, all of you! If we all do what we are supposed to do, and carry out orders correctly, we will have a new chief of state by nightfall. But if we continue to think of the past, we will fail again.

TIGER: (Passionately.) Talk, talk, talk! Every time we meet, talk, talk, talk!

EXECUTOR: That is not so. Three times our department nearly brought us our war with the Reds. In 1960, '61 and '62. However ...

LION: Wait a minute! You said three times. I've never heard of it.

EXECUTOR: Does the right hand know what the left hand is doing? Did the mugger tell Paul about Peter? In the Agency, Lion, are so many damn departments that all of them are falling over each other. You know that.

Lion: I know that, but this is the first time I have heard of three near misses.

EXECUTOR: Well, at the time they occurred you were not high enough on the ladder. However, I will now show how close we were to prove to our two friends here (nods toward the TWO CUBANS) how close we really came.

DANCER: Yes, señor, I would like to know how your, I beg your pardon, how OUR country nearly came to blows with the Reds.

EXECUTOR: Don't get sarcastic, Dancer. The first time was the U-2 incident when we compelled Mr. K[19] to scrub the Paris Conference.

TIGER: We were not even close to war when that happened.

EXECUTOR: Are you sure? Have you forgotten that we sent another U-2 into Russia near the Turkish border? Have you all forgotten the red alert? What if some trigger-happy brass dropped a few bombs at that time?

LION: Well, that is the first one, but where was the second one?

EXECUTOR: Why, the Bay of Pigs, of course. My God, how much closer can you provoke a nation into war? We committed sabotage by agents trained and paid by us. We bombed the island with pilots and bombs; we gave and paid for both of them. We trained and paid for an entire invasion force. We transported this army, supplied them with all types of weapons,

---

[19] "Mr. K": Nikita Khrushchev, premier of the Soviet Union from 1958 to 1964.

and paid for their services. Do you think that the Soviets would have stood by if we did that to their territory? Of course not.

DANCER: What went wrong? Was the chief of state scared?

EXECUTOR: Hell, no. He found out that the Agency was feeding him a lot of crap. But what really turned the scale was the fact that he received information about the "blood list."

LION: Blood list? What was that?

EXECUTOR: Oh, that was a phrase first used by the Nazi Gestapo. Any German who opposed Hitler before he came into power was placed on a Nazi list that enumerated the people he wanted executed. To obtain the services of the Batista group they permitted that group to make up lists of Cubans who would be killed if the invasion had succeeded.

TIGER: Well, that should happen to all traitors.

EXECUTOR: Would you pull the trigger to kill 77,000 Cubans, Tiger?

LION: Good God, 77,000 people were on the kill list?

EXECUTOR: That is just what the chief of state said when he was informed of the "blood list." He could understand the shooting of the key man in the administration of the Bearded One, but the chief is not a butcher. That is one of the unpublicized reasons why the chief refused to order the airplanes into the island when the invasion faltered and then collapsed.

LION: Was that the only reason?

EXECUTOR: No. Another reason was the fact that the Agency had imprisoned every anti-Batista leader on the day we invaded the island. In addition, we had also imprisoned all Cubans in the invasion army who refused to serve under the Batista followers who were made officers of the invasion army. If the invasion had succeeded and those men returned to the island they also would have been murdered. If he permitted that to occur you can well imagine the revulsion that would have swept over the world.

DANCER: Let's get on with our plan. What is the ne...

LION: Wait a minute! That is only two occasions. What about the third?

EXECUTOR: The Missile Crisis, of course! This country was less than eight hours away from a war with the Reds.

TIGER: Don't feed us that crap. Eight hours? Boloney. The Reds were so scared, they pulled out at the first sight of blood.

EXECUTOR: No, you missed the point, because you do not have the facts. What you do not know was that on the second or third day of the crisis, the EIA ordered a U-2 flight deep into Siberia. The pilot was directed to eject himself when he was as near as possible to the Red naval base at Vladivostok. On him were papers showing the location of our Seventh Fleet approaching that base, and the time of a strike by the carrier planes of the Seventh Fleet.

LION: What happened?

EXECUTOR: Someone got cold feet, and the chief of state was notified. He ordered the U-2 to return to the U-2 base immediately and, at the same time, he personally telephoned the Red ambassador that the flight was a mistake. Within two hours, the plane was on its way back to its Alaskan base.

TIGER: That seemed childish. Was that the Agency's war plan?

EXECUTOR: Of course not. The plan was a plan to go to war, and there is a tremendous difference. If you were the Red commander at the Vladivostok naval base and you saw a plane capable of carrying a nuclear bomb, what would you think? Remember, Tiger, this is the second or third day of the confrontation, and the Reds have seen partial mobilization in the continental United States and full mobilization elsewhere. Now, put yourself in the shoes or mind of the Red commander. What would you think?

TIGER: Under those conditions the plane was going to try and knock the base out. But then, what caused the Red to hesitate?

EXECUTOR: That man was no fool. He quickly saw that only one plane was on his radar screens and that there were no follow-up planes. So, he merely sent up a flight of Red aircraft to escort the U-2 back toward our country. However, if the Agency had been able to send four or more planes into Red territory, they would have been compelled to shoot them down. Can you imagine what our fearless press would have said? That is how close we came.

LION: I never did understand that confrontation between us and the Reds. International law upheld our position all the time.

The Reds have no sea power to transport men and material to invade us. It was a fool's gambit.

EXECUTOR: No, it was not a fool's gambit. As a matter of international law, any nation can purchase any type of weapon it so desires. Whether or not another nation will permit the purchase of those weapons is not international law but power. International law is always interpreted by those who have the guns to make the interpretation stick. If we have the right to give weapons to all the nations bordering on the Soviet Union, why shouldn't they have the right to give weapons to countries bordering our land?

DANCER: For Christ's sake, that's water over the dam. Let's get on with it.

EXECUTOR: Yes, you are right. The plan will go into operation on the twenty-second. Okay, Lion, take over.

LION: Since the announcement in the Dallas newspapers on the twenty-third of September, I have gone over the route he will use. We have obtained the route data from our friends in the police department.

Now, here are the maps and photographs. (LION picks up a briefcase and places it on table.) I have also brought along a slide projector so that all of us can see what is involved. Tiger, will you please get the projector and screen?

(TIGER rises and goes to the front hallway through the right rear door. He reenters carrying a slide projector and screen.

The window drapes are drawn during this scene, just prior to the dimming of the stage lights. The drawing of the drapes should, if possible, synchronize with the dimming of the stage lights. The slide projector must be able to cast a sharply defined picture and be capable of casting one at least eight feet high.

The screen should be placed in the middle of the stage so that it can be seen by everyone in the audience. An electrical outlet should be on the left front of the stage where the lamp of the room is connected. This makes the scene more natural.

As Tiger puts the screen in place and is carrying the screen toward the dining table:)

EXECUTOR: Fellows, move the table over here and take the chairs away so we can all see.

(LION, DANCER, PILOT, and MARINE each take hold of a table corner and place it where EXECUTOR has pointed. The table should be lifted carefully since the whiskey, glasses, and fruit are upon it. After the table is in place, TIGER puts the slide projector on the table and attaches the cord to the wall socket. He steps away. As he steps away, MARINE goes to the drapes and pulls them close and the lights grow dim.

LION places in the projector a map, which he takes from the briefcase, that was published in the *Dallas News* on the morning of November 22, 1963, which shows no detours.

All actors are now standing near the left side of the table.)

Tiger: (Using a long pointer which he has picked up from the couch.) The chief of state's motorcade will come south on Main Street, cross Houston Street, and continue on Main Street until he goes under and past this triple underpass. I don't like it. I do not want to commit suicide. Where the hell is my protection?

DANCER: I agree. You're asking me to be in the open with rifles in our hands. You want us to be lynched? That open area is crazy!

EXECUTOR: Now, don't get excited. Lion is showing you the area surrounding the cavalcade. Put on the slide showing the buildings, Lion.

(LION removes the map slide and inserts the slide showing the buildings on Houston and Elm Streets. This is the USIA[20] photo or any photograph showing those buildings.)

MARINE: (Raises hand.) Sir.

EXECUTOR: What is it, Marine?

MARINE: I see two excellent places. The warehouse building, say from the second or third floor windows, behind the fire escape. The other one at the wooden fence at the top of the hill. The warehouse building is perfect, since it would give the rifle-man plenty of time to aim. But more important would be the fact that the rifleman in the warehouse could not be seen by anyone on the street or in the other corner building.

EXECUTOR: I see that you have learned more than just Russian and secret codes while in the Corps. But why not use the depository?

MARINE: Well, sir, there are probably a lot of workers in the depository, and they will be using the windows to watch him go by. In addition, how could a rifleman get the rifle into the building without being seen? Hell, the SSB is supposed to be guarding all buildings along any route used by a chief of state.

---

[20] The United States Information Agency.

LION: That guarding business is all a myth. The Bureau does not have the manpower, so that job is up to the local police. We all know how much the Dallas Police love the chief.

MARINE: But that still does not answer the question of how the rifle is taken into the building. Christ, to top it off, the rifleman has to carry it from a hiding place to the window, with workers all over the place. No, I say it can't be done.

EXECUTOR: Well, you may ...

MARINE: Wait a minute. I have just thought of something. How the hell would the rifleman know the EXACT time the chief of state will appear in his telescopic site? There is never any radio broadcast of his exact location during his automobile ride.

EXECUTOR: Forget about the rifle, for I will personally take care of it. Marine, from the depository, say from the fifth or sixth-floor windows, could a rifleman hit a man, fatally, in a moving car?

MARINE: (Approaches the screen. Are there any trees on Houston Street?

LION: No, it would be a clear shot.

MARINE: It could be done. You know that my service record showed how lousy I was on the range. No, I doubt that one shot could do it. That is why I favor a cross-fire ambush. Now (MARINE now uses pointer while he talks), if you look closely, once the chief's auto proceeds down Elm Street he cannot turn back; he must go forward and pass the wooden fence at the top of the hill. This gives a rifleman at that spot at least ten seconds to draw a bead and shoot. And the rifleman in the warehouse could also have a clear shot. That is how I would set it up.

LION: Lion, I still like the depository.

EXECUTOR: No! He's absolutely right. A rifleman in the depository must use the sixth floor to shoot between the branches of the tree. But if there is the slightest amount of wind, the branches' movement will distract any rifleman. Marine is also correct regarding the warehouse, as a rifleman there will have a good sixty seconds to continue firing while the chief's automobile seeks to get out of range. We will use both the warehouse and the wooden [fence]. This time, I want all the odds in our favor. Once the chief is on Elm Street he is dead, dead, dead!

PILOT: Marine did bring up a point.

EXECUTOR: Speak up, Pilot, speak up. We want everything that can help us.

PILOT: Well, we could use the depository as a diversionary tactic. Why not give the impression that the shots were fired from that building? Why not hide a rifle in a place someone would look to find it? Or leave some expanded cartridges that cannot fit the rifle? Boy, that would create confusion!

LION: By God, it's perfect! Absolutely perfect. What do you think, sir?

EXECUTOR: Yes, it is excellent. We can embellish here and there; and, with some assistance from our friends in Dallas, we can create a smokescreen that will blur the facts. Yes, we will do it.

DANCER: What I hear is very good. But everyone is not seeing the forest because of the trees.

TIGER: What do you mean?

DANCER: How can we make the chief's automobile come down Houston and then turn down Elm? The map shows the parade going straight down Main. So, I ask you, how do you get him to go down Elm? (While talking, DANCER is using the pointer.)

LION: He is right. Without those two detours the plan is dead.

EXECUTOR: No, the plan will not be abolished. Since the success of the plan depends upon a double detour, we will have a double detour.

PILOT: By God, our department must have one hell of a lot of influence with the SSB to compel them to change a route plan. Jesus, can you imagine the questions the Bureau will ask of you after the assassination? I would not want to be in your shoes for all the tea in China!

EXECUTOR: Who said anything about obtaining SSB permission? I simply said the route will be changed. It is not a question of influence but merely the use of human psychology. For example, Pilot, say a few men in a city street repair truck drove up to the front of this home, right now, and started to tear up the street with jackhammers or with pick and shovel. Would you go out and ask them who gave them permission to do what they are doing? Of course not.

Pilots. So?

EXECUTOR: So, on the morning of the twenty-second, a couple of our men, driving a Dallas city street repair truck, will simply put up wooden horse barricades at Main and Houston, and also at Houston and Elm. The lead car, which carries the police and the Secret Service, will just follow directions and *booinng!* (Snapping fingers.)

LION: But won't the SSB or the Dallas Police lead auto know what is wrong?

EXECUTOR: Hell, no. The crowd will have formed around those barricades, and each department will believe that the other approved the route. This is merely applying human nature. Forget your worries.

LION: Then, sir, we go ahead?

EXECUTOR: In my opinion, yes. Do you all agree?

(All nod heads "yes." LION rises, pours out drink in each glass. They all rise and toast each other, silently, drink it down and reseat themselves. The slide projector is turned off and the screen raised. Both are removed by TIGER, who takes them near the window. As the drapes are opened the stage lights grow brighter. MARINE, PILOT, DANCER, and TIGER move table to original spot. The actors remain standing.)

LION: All right everyone, I want Marine and Pilot to remain while the rest of you go out for some lunch. Dancer and Tiger, you meet with us in about two hours at the warehouse.

EXECUTOR: Wait a moment. LION forgot to show you something. Show them in.

(LION walks to rear right door, opens it, and motions with hand. In walk two men, dressed in the identical clothes worn by MARINE, hair combed the same way, and the same height and build. They walk only about ten feet into room, stop and face the others.)

CUBANS: It can't be! Three of them! What's up?

EXECUTOR: Yes, these two men look like Marine. They are decoys chosen to protect us and him. At no time will any one of you speak to anyone of them unless they speak to you first. That's an order!

(EXECUTOR waves his hand to THE TWO NEW ACTORS who turn and walk out of door, closing it behind them.)

Now, Tiger, Dancer, both of you may leave and I'll see you in two hours. Oh, by the way, Tiger, I again thank you.

(The two CUBANS shake hands with PILOT and MARINE, bow to EXECUTOR, and leave by rear right door, shutting it as they depart. EXECUTOR, PILOT, MARINE, and LION resume their seats.)

EXECUTOR: Pilot, I am going to keep you for just a few minutes. On the twentieth of next month I want you to go to

Dallas with Marine Number Two. On the outskirts of Dallas is a small airfield and I want you to try and rent a plane, with long-range potential, for use on the twenty-second. Be sure and stress the fact that you want it for a long-range flight. The Marine Number Two will not speak at all but take you with a woman who can speak both English and Spanish. If the operator asks for a deposit give it to him. If he refuses, just walk away.

PILOT: Why all this?

EXECUTOR: To give the impression that the Bearded One is involved. A "Red" herring, so to speak.

Pilot: Is that all?

EXECUTOR: Yes. The following day, the twenty-first, you are to leave Dallas and travel around a bit. Do not return to Dallas. That is all you are to do, unless you receive further personal instructions from me. Any questions? (PILOT shakes head "no.") Okay then, that's all.

(PILOT rises, shakes hands with all, and walks out door. After Pilot has closed door, EXECUTOR pours himself a drink, motions to both Marine and Lion to help themselves. Patsy shakes head "no" but Lion pours himself a drink. Both drinkers then drink and place the glass down on table.)

EXECUTOR: Well, Marine, this is what you have been waiting for, a crack at one of our enemies. Since you have been with the Department way back in Japan, we have been pleased by your progress.

MARINE: Well, sir, I have tried to do my duty. I am pleased to be accepted.

EXECUTOR: You know that you will be only a decoy, a Patsy, so to speak?

MARINE: I know that but I also know that the Department will protect me.

EXECUTOR: Before we go any further, Marine, what went wrong in Russia?

MARINE: In my opinion someone in the Department snafued[21] but good.

EXECUTOR: I do not understand. Who snafued? Please explain for I want to know.

MARINE: If you recall, the Department had me apply for a passport to Russia while I was still wearing the uniform. That was on fourth of September in '59. Then when I received the passport on September tenth, the very next day some bastard transferred me from the Active to Inactive Reserve. And to top it off, I was shoved onto a boat ten days later, in spite of the fact I received a hardship discharge.

EXECUTOR: I still do not understand, for I see nothing wrong.

MARINE: Nothing wrong, sir? Goddamn it, if you were a Red you could spot it immediately. You know I had a Class A

[21] Snafu: U.S. military slang from 1941; an acronym for "Situation Normal, All Fucked Up."

security clearance in the Corps. Well, when I was transferred some stupid bastard forgot to remove me from Class A security clearance. So, Mr. Executor, how could I be an honest-to-God defector if I was still on the Class A security list of the Corps?

EXECUTOR: Jesus Christ, what monumental stupidity! The Commies knew you were a phony as long as you were on that list. By the way, I received reports that you were quite a shot with a rifle.

MARINE: (Laughing.) Now, I know you must be kidding. I made so many "Maggie's drawers"[22] in the Corps that the guys kept kidding me to open up a womens wear store and call it "Maggie's Drawers." (All laugh.) Well, I really was worried while in Russia. I honestly believed that I was stuck there forever.

LION: That is what is called a quid pro quo!

MARINE: What's that?

LION: Latin, something for something, an exchange of equal value. In this game, Marine, each side may do something for a mutual favor. It is like a promissory note. You give us our agent now and sometime in the future when [we] capture one of yours we will return him. Like the Powers-Able exchange in '61. If we did not play by the rules, Marine, each side would soon be

---

[22] U.S. Army slang dating back to the 1930s. According to Merriam-Webster, it alludes to "The red flag waved across the target by a marker on the target range when a shot has completely missed the target."

out of business. And if that ever happens I'll be out of a job. And who in the hell would ever hire me?
(All laugh.)

EXECUTOR: All right, all right. Back to business. Now, Marine, we have created a background to convince the public that you are a fervent Red who admires everything and everyone who is a Red.

MARINE: You can say that again. I found that every time you mention the word "Red" in this country, the entire country has a bowel movement. Man, when that happens, it raises a hell of a stink!

EXECUTOR: Did you order the rifle last March as directed?

MARINE: Yes, sir. I ordered one with a telescopic site but with no ammunition. In addition, to play it safe, I ordered a rifle from a coupon that carried a different list price. Then I had it sent to my PO Box in Dallas but with a money order under a different name.

EXECUTOR: Good, good. How is its condition?

MARINE: (In astonishment.) How the hell do I know? I don't even know if the Chicago firm sent it out. I never received it, you know that.

EXECUTOR: (Laughing.) I was just testing you. We know you never received it and there is no proof that you received it. However, does your wife know that you have a rifle?

MARINE: Yes, sir, she does. I purchased a rifle last January and she has seen it around the house. But, as instructed, I have never used it under any circumstance. That one has no telescopic site on it.

EXECUTOR: Excellent. Now, Marine, we have arranged a job for you at the book depository. It does not pay much so the Department will supplement your wages by another twenty dollars every week. You are to arrange to have a room in a boarding house during the work week to save money.

LION: In this job, Marine, you are to reverse your role you had in the Corps. No brawls and no spouting off about how good the Reds are. The industrious and polite. Understood?

(MARINE nods "yes.")

MARINE: What do I do on the twenty-second?

EXECUTOR: No, first I want you to visit your family in Irving on the twenty-first, sleep there, and ride back with a fellow employee who we know lives next door. Now, Marine, you will need some kind of a package to carry into the depository on the twenty-second. There must be something in that package that you honestly need. Have any idea?

MARINE: I know one. My room could use a set of curtains. The shade has holes in it and when it is up, or down, everyone on the street can look in. I could go out and buy some curtain rods.

EXECUTOR: Very good but make sure that your next-door neighbors in Irving see you have the package on Friday morning. If they ask you what is in it, tell the truth, curtain rods.

MARINE: Yes, sir.

EXECUTOR: Now, Marine, listen very carefully. On the twenty-second be sure that you are seen by some of the employees during your lunch time. Talk to them but be seen. When you hear or see the chief's automobile nearing the depository, go outside and stand at the entrance.

MARINE: Why?

EXECUTOR: Why? Because that is going to be your unimpeachable alibi!

MARINE: I don't, I don't understand.

LION: Neither do I.

EXECUTOR: I can see that neither of you understand human nature. What do a great many people do when attending a parade of the chief of state?

(MARINE and LION look at each other, shrugging their shoulders.)

EXECUTOR: What a pair of idiots! Pictures, they take pictures. Now do you see what I'm driving at?

(Again MARINE and LION shrug shoulders.)

EXECUTOR: Idiots! Everyone is taking pictures, including the press and television cameraman. What is more normal than the employees of a building standing outside the building's steps to watch him go by? So, I'll bet a million to one that Marine will be in someone's picture and on film.

MARINE: Holy cow! A picture alibi!

EXECUTOR: A picture alibi. For how can Marine be the rifleman, if, at the time the shots are fired, he is seen in photographs or on film, standing at the entrance of the depository?

LION: I bow (stands up and vows to EXECUTOR) to you.

MARINE: Okay. So I'm in pictures. But then what do I do?

EXECUTOR: Go back into the building and hang around the first or second floor. Try and be seen and then leave the building. Near the east end of the plaza you will see a green station wagon driven by one of our men. He will leave you off at your boarding room around 1:00 p.m. When you hear our signal go outside and we will have you picked up and driven around until you have to enter the theater. There you will be picked up by the cops. We have your revolver so do not be surprised if you see it at the police station.

MARINE: Do I carry a gun with me?

EXECUTOR: No, for if you do you're liable to be knocked off. So, play it cool.

Marine: And at the police station?

EXECUTOR: Oh, they'll knock you around a bit. You keep saying that you killed no one. Now, Marine, as to a lawyer. I want you to ask for that New York lawyer who was always defending "left-wingers." The press will play it up big and this will reinforce the impression that you are a dyed-in-the-wool Red.

MARINE: Will the lawyer represent me?

EXECUTOR: Hell, no! He won't even receive a phone call from Dallas.

MARINE: But I do get a lawyer, don't I?

EXECUTOR: Of course. Do you think the Department will let you down? Have we in the past?

MARINE: No, you have always protected me.

LION: But what if the police ask him to take a lie test?

EXECUTOR: He takes it! Gladly. Willingly! Why, the needle will not even quiver. Did you shoot the chief? No. Did you purchase a rifle? Yes. Did you use the rifle to murder the chief? No. Do you know who shot the chief of state? No. Where were you when the shots were fired? Why, on the steps of the building. When did you purchase a rifle? Last February. Did a telescopic sight come with it? No. Did you have a revolver when arrested? No. See the point, Marine?

MARINE: Jesus! That is perfect. Every answer I give is the truth.

Lion: AGAIN I bow (stand up and bow to EXECUTOR) to genius!

EXECUTOR: (Stands up, so does MARINE as LION remains standing.) All right, Marine, I will not see you for some time. Follow instructions and nothing will go wrong. Your patriotism will be rewarded. Good luck.

(EXECUTOR SHAKES hands with MARINE and then LION. MARINE leaves and closes door behind him.)

LION: There goes a brave man!

EXECUTOR: You mean there goes a stupid son of a bitch!

Lion: That's a hell of a crack to make. Why?

EXECUTOR: Why, because he's stupid. Do you think the Department has forgotten that he tried to commit suicide, and failed, while in Russia? He will crack wide open. You don't think for a minute that we would let him go on trial? How asinine do you think we are? Oh, he will play his part to perfection, but to us he is nothing more than our great, big, beautiful patsy. And in this game, as you know, Lion, the only good patsy is a dead one. Come on, let us go out and have some lunch and then meet with the other two characters.

CURTAIN

End of Act II, Scene I.

Act II, Scene II: "The Planting of the Idea."

TIME: Same day; later afternoon.

STAGE SETTING: The stage for this scene is an exact replica of the sixth floor of the Texas School Book Depository as shown in the official photographs released by the Warren Commission. This is the "shield of cartons" which, the Commission alleged, was used by the "sole and exclusive killer" of President John F. Kennedy.

Book cartons are scattered all over the floor and from these cartons Dancer and Tiger will construct the "shield" which was done in real life by two of the conspirators approximately ten minutes before the shooting and completing their task within twenty-five minutes. That two men did, in fact and in law, construct this shield can be found in a testimony of witnesses before the Commission.

The main action of the two actors is to construct the shield before the eyes of the audience. Therefore, there MUST be weight in the twenty-five to thirty cartons lifted by these two actors. The average weight per carton, according to the Commission, was approximately fifty pounds; so if the actors show a little sweat it will do no harm.

The producer or stage director must remember that the shield, according to the photograph, had two rows, the row nearest the windows being only half as high as the second row which is approximately six feet high. There are cartons lined up high against the left wall, and the director must have cartons laying around at random on the floor. It will be the random cartons that are used to construct the shield.

At the rear of the stage are windows, as shown in the photograph, and the left window is the one from which, allegedly, the killer fired his three shots.

THE PROPS: Cartons, two rifles with telescopic sights attached, and a knife.

ACTORS: EXECUTOR, LION, DANCER, TIGER.

CLOTHES: CUBANS in blue jeans, T-shirts. AMERICANS in same clothes as in Scene I.

(EXECUTOR and LION are standing near front center stage. DANCER and TIGER are near the windows, looking out.)

EXECUTOR: All right, men, let's get going. Gather round. (The two CUBANS come to where EXECUTOR and LION are standing. All then sit down on cartons in a semi-circle, facing each other.)
Tiger, Dancer, you two have been selected to create the "smoke screen." Both of you are strong and agile and know how to work fast under pressure. This floor has the same layout as the sixth floor in the depository. But as we all know now, the chances of making a clean fatal hit from those windows (EXECUTOR points to them) are pretty small. So, we are simply going to use the sixth floor as a "Red" herring.

DANCER: Then no shots will be fired from that floor?

EXECUTOR: Right. The rifleman's angle of fire from those windows is too difficult to secure one hundred percent accuracy. We cannot afford to fail.

TIGER: What do you want us to do?

EXECUTOR: Both of you are to make a shield of cartons to give the impression that a rifleman used the shield to protect himself from the prying eyes of the building employees. In other words, a hiding place.

TIGER: Then the shield will have to be at least six feet high.

EXECUTOR: Correct.

DANCER: How much time do we have?

EXECUTOR: Our investigation revealed the fact that some of the black employees use the sixth floor as a lunch room. That is from 12:00 noon to about 12:20 or 12:25, when they must go down and punch the time clock. So, that means you will have about twenty-five minutes.

DANCER: Jeez, I don't know. That seems kinda close to lift and carry thirty to thirty-five cartons.

LION: Oh, crap! Quit griping, Dancer, there are two of you, which means that each one of you carry about seventeen to eighteen cartons. Hell, after practicing a bit, I'll bet you get it down to about fifteen or twenty minutes. What the hell, we're not going to give you a gold medal for construction work.

TIGER: It still looks too damn close.

LION: No, it is not. We know the chief of state is scheduled to arrive at his luncheon at 1:00. By using the SSB procedure we know his automobile will be in your area at about 12:25, give or take a few minutes. Do not forget that we will have help from some Dallas ...

EXECUTOR: Hold on! It's none of their goddamn business what we do. They have only one job to do. Keep it that way.

LION: I'm sorry.

DANCER: Is that all we do, simply construct a shield?

EXECUTOR: No, you will also plant some evidence for the police to find.

DANCER: What evidence?

EXECUTOR: A 7.65 German Mauser with a telescopic sight and some spent cartridges. You will hide the rifle where it can be easily found.

TIGER: Rifle! What rifle? What the hell are you talking about? How the hell are Dancer and I going to take a rifle into the building on the day of the murder? What are you, nuts?

EXECUTOR: Like a squirrel. Who said anything about you bringing a rifle into the depository? I said you were going to plant and hide one.

TIGER: (Sputtering.) But, but, but, but..

EXECUTOR: Oh, quit acting like a motorboat. There will be a German Mauser rifle on the sixth floor. You will have in your pocket three spent cartridges, one of which will be deformed, and the other three unable to be ballistically matched to the

Mauser. After you have completed the shield, you gently throw the three cartridges near the window.

TIGER: Wait a minute. Just wait a minute. You have not answered my question. Where will the rifle be if we do not have it with us?

EXECUTOR: Like Poe's "Purloined Letter," in sight but not seen.

TIGER: Goddamn it! Now, we get riddles. Well, give us the answer.

EXECUTOR: Stand easy! Stand easy. (Points to two cartons lying near the right middle of the stage. These cartons are "Books" with a white stripe running through the word "Books." The cartons are in a vertical upright position.)

EXECUTOR: Tiger, open up one of those cartons.

(EXECUTOR points to cartons. TIGER goes over to a carton, pulls out switchblade knife, opens blade, and cuts top of carton through the middle. He pulls up the flaps and commences to pull out books which drop onto the floor. TIGER stops, looks up at EXECUTOR, who gives a smile as TIGER slowly pulls out a German Mauser rifle with a telescopic sight attached. The rifle also has a black-brown sling. The rifle must be packed diagonally within the carton.)

DANCER: Jesus Christ!

LION: Sir, if you keep pulling these acts of genius out of your pockets, I will be bent over permanently. (LION bows to EXECUTOR.)

EXECUTOR: (Speaking in a pleased, smiling voice.) Rise, Sir Lion, I do know my business.

TIGER: But how will we know what carton to open?

EXECUTOR: It will be marked in the identical manner like the one you opened. Remember, both of you, that after you take the rifle out of the carton, you must replace the books and stand it on its end, like this. (EXECUTIVE walks over and shows what he wants to be done.) Now, Tiger, open up the other carton.

(TIGER lays down rifle on a carton. TIGER walks over to other carton pointed to by EXECUTOR and repeats performance. Here he removes a 6.5 Italian Mannlicher-Carcano rifle, but with no telescopic site attached.)

DANCER: Good God! Another one!

EXECUTOR: Not quite. Dancer, please open up that other small carton. (DANCER repeats performance and removes a telescopic sight. Now TIGER has the Italian rifle in his hands; the sight in DANCER's.)

LION: Why two?

EXECUTOR: Lion, examine the Italian rifle and tell us what you find.

LION: (Takes Italian rifle from DANCER.) Well, this one says "Made in Italy, 6.5 Caliber." (LION opens rifle and peers down into the gun barrel.) My God, sir, this barrel is corroded. (Pulls trigger.) Why, the firing pin is dented. If anyone tries to fire this rifle it could blow up in his face. Here, Dancer (gives rifle to Dancer), let me see that scope. (DANCER gives telescopic site to LION, who looks through it.) What the hell, this damn scope is structurally defective. (Now LION gives the rifle back to DANCER, takes rifle from DANCER, and attempts to place telescopic sight on the rifle.)

Mr. Executor, this sight does not fit on the rifle. It needs two or three shims so that it can be used properly. In fact, the scope can only be used by a left-handed rifleman. Hell, this Italian rifle is worthless; it's nothing but a piece of junk! (Puts rifle and telescopic site on another carton.)

DANCER: Mr. Executor, what rifle do we plant?

EXECUTOR: Why should you know? Just hide the one you find in the carton. Both of you must wear light five-fingered gloves so as not to leave fingerprints. One other thing, do not pull the trigger on the rifle, for there will be a live bullet in it. So, be careful.

TIGER: Why can't we know what rifle will be in the carton?

EXECUTOR: The less you know, the safer you will be. But I will say that what the police say regarding the rifle they find on the sixth floor will not be the one they will find. The rifle you do not plant will be used at the proper time and place.

(EXECUTOR now walks, by himself, to the window, gazes around as if studying the floor and the various measurements. Walks back to the other three.)

EXECUTOR: Now, I want both of you to build a shield of cartons. To save time, I have drawn a sketch and we'll walk through it.

(EXECUTOR draws out a white folded piece of paper, shows it to the two men, and they proceed to construct the shield. The two CUBANS do not touch the cartons on the left side of the stage, nor the cartons already in position on the right wall. They use only those cartons lying on the floor. As the shield is being constructed, LION and EXECUTOR keep glancing at their wristwatches. When finished, the actors stand aside so that the audience can see the shield. This shield must be an exact duplicate of the official photograph published by the Warren Commission.)

EXECUTOR: (After the completion of the shield.) Good. Just like I want it.

LION: No, sir! Something is out of whack.

DANCER: I see nothing wrong.

LION: Look closely. Tell me how the alleged rifleman gets in and out of the shield. Look at the height and then look at both ends of the shield. There is no entrance and no exit! Why, the man would have to be the world's greatest standing high-jumper.

EXECUTOR: No, let them make the shield just like it stands now. That will present a nice puzzle to the police.

TIGER: What do we do with the rifle?

EXECUTOR: (Takes rifle with telescopic sight.) After you have finished with the shield, put the rifle between the two rows of cartons. (EXECUTOR walks over to cartons and shows them, then brings rifle back to original carton and lays it on that carton.)

Dancer: Everything looks fine, but how do we get in and out of the building?

EXECUTOR: Both of you enter the building around 10:30 in the morning. The building has offices on every floor leased by various businesses. Wear business suits and no one will question you, since it is open to the public. I would take the elevator to the fourth or fifth floor and walk up to the seventh floor. Then stay there until 12:20 or 12:25 and walk down and get to work. If any Blacks come up to the sixth floor to eat, you will have to wait until they leave to punch the time clock downstairs. But they will be gone by 12:20 or 12:25 at the latest. Now, be sure to close the carton that has the rifle in it and also be sure that the carton is mixed up with the others. After finishing that, go back up to the seventh floor and wait.

DANCER: We wait how long?

LION: Until you decide it's safe to come down.

TIGER: But we would be taking a chance someone will see us. What if the building is sealed off?

LION: No chance at all. Everyone will be rushing outside to see the commotion. The building has four or five exits, on the side and in the rear. However, to play it safe, we will furnish both of you with authentic press passes from a Cuban American newspaper. If the police stop you, just show them the pass. Be sure and memorize the paper's phone number and its editor.

TIGER: I was thinking that Dancer and me ought to practice up here. Is that okay with you?

EXECUTOR: Sure. But leave that for the day after tomorrow. We have to use this floor for something else. Now, I want both of you to break up the shield. Replace those rifles. Well, any questions?

DANCER: Yes, sir. How will you get the rifle in the carton into the building?

EXECUTOR: Tiger, we have friends in many places. Well, good luck. (Laughing.)

(EXECUTOR and LION walk out the right rear door as TIGER and DANCER commence to take the cartons down from the shield.)

CURTAIN

End of Act II, Scene II.

Act II, Scene III: "Two Out of Three."

TIME: The following morning.

PLACE: The warehouse.

CAST: Executor, Lion, Bulldog, Hawk.

PROPS: Cartons at random, as in Act II, Scene II. No rifles, no knife.

A three-section eight-foot easel. The easels display the photographs showing the entire area of Dealey Plaza, the streets and buildings on Main, Elm, and Houston Street.

The easels are in three sections and must have good support so that the actors can easily assemble the sections before the eyes of the audience. The easels are placed on the left side of the stage wall, on the edge, not laid flat. The stage is thus the same as in Scene II.

CURTAIN

EXECUTOR and LION are each sitting on a carton, smoking. The rear door at the right opens; in walk two new actors: HAWK and BULLDOG. Both are dressed in casual sports clothes, Cuban style.

BULLDOG: Right on time, sir.

EXECUTOR: Good. In this business I value men who know the meaning of time. Draw up a carton and sit down. (Both do so.)

Both of you know why you are here? (Both nod "yes.") If anything goes wrong, you realize the penalty? (Both nod "yes.") Now I want to know, here and now, if either of you have any objections. Do you, Bulldog? (Shakes head "no.") Do you, Hawk? (Shakes head "no.") All right. We hit him on the twenty-second of next month.

HAWK: I was ready a long time ago, but you called it off.

BULLDOG: Well, we're here, let's get on with it. What is the plan?

EXECUTOR: Both of you will shoot at him from behind the fence at the top of the hill. Here, give us a hand and I'll show you.

(EXECUTOR followed by LION; and then HAWK and BULLDOG go over to the easels, pick them up, and bring them to the proper place at the middle front of the stage. When finally assembled, EXECUTOR holds a long piece of wood, slim, in his hand and uses it to outline the ambush area. The actors, naturally, stand aside so as not to block the view.)

You will both have clear shots at the chief as his auto passes by. His car will be coming down toward you on Elm Street, then pass you as he continues under the triple underpass. Once he turns onto Elm Street and proceeds past the depository, he will be in your sights all the way.

EXECUTOR: What about the cops and the wives?

The service SOP[23] is to have the chief sit on the right rear seat, with the governor sitting on the jump seat. The wives sit next to them. As for cops, there will be two or three flank guard to the auto.

BULLDOG: Will the bubble be up?

EXECUTOR: That I do not know. If the weather is clear it will not be used. Of course, if the bubble is used the operation is off.

HAWK: Will those cops be able to ride up that hill leading to the fence?

EXECUTOR: No, their cycles cannot take the incline. We have already tested that problem on our exercise grounds, so you have no worry. Don't forget, people will be running all over the area and this will hinder the cops from reaching your area. Lion, you take over.

LION: (Using pointer taken from EXECUTOR:) This is where both of you will be when you fire the shots. As you can see, once the chief's auto is on Elm Street he cannot turn back. He must proceed forward, and this will give you about fifteen to twenty seconds to aim and fire.

HAWK: How many shots do we fire?

LION: For God's sake, how do I know? You fellows are pulling the trigger. I do not have to tell you how to do your job. You've done this type of work before; that's why you were chosen.

---

[23] SOP: Standard operating procedure.

BULLDOG: When do we start shooting?

EXECUTOR: When you hear a shot!

BULLDOG: A shot! What shot? What the hell are you talking about? I thought we were the only ones involved. Now, we get a partner.

EXECUTOR: Well, you thought wrong. Do you think we would let this opportunity slip by? Events are catching up to us. We have discovered that the chief has sent a secret agent to open negotiations with the Bearded One. He is attempting a détente with the Reds. His feelers with the various Red nations to obtain some sort of peace, a "live and let live" attitude, does not appeal to us and to various sectors of our economy. Internally, there's too damn much socialism. So, we believe he must go, and go he will.

HAWK: I'm not interested in the reasons. Why the extra man?

EXECUTOR: I told you that this operation would be a cross-fire ambush. We are simply making sure that everything goes right.

BULLDOG: Where will this other man be? Do we know him? Does he know us?

LION: Now, you know better than to ask. The answer is no to all of them. I can tell you this. The other rifleman will be in another building that will give him a forty to fifty-degree angle of fire. He will be firing at the chief when his auto is about twenty-five to thirty-five feet on Elm Street. Thus, in back of him will be two or three other automobiles, thus preventing his driver from driving backwards. Both of you will be firing at angles between twenty to thirty degrees. You will hit him from the front and side, the other man from the back.

BULLDOG: Well, I don't want to be behind that fence too long. Someone is bound to see us and I want out, fast. So, what is the plan?

EXECUTOR: You know we leave nothing to chance. On the morning of the twenty-second you will find a green station wagon at our garage. In the glove compartment you will find auto and driver's licenses for both of you under other names. Beneath the floorboard will be a new golf bag, and in it will be two rifles with telescopic sights. In the bag's ball pocket will be the ammunition.

HAWK: How good are those rifles?

EXECUTOR: (Laughing.) Hawk, those rifles are the best any millionaire can buy. Every part has been tested. As a matter of fact, both of you have been using the type of rifles that will be in the bag. Don't worry, just get him in your sights and pull the trigger.

HAWK: I don't see any difficulty. Do you, Bulldog?

BULLDOG: No, no trouble. But what about our getaway?

EXECUTOR: (Turning toward LION.) What about the plans? That is your department.

LION: Simplicity is the plan. Both of them will be dressed in hunting clothes, since in Dallas at that time of the year many men walk around the streets in them. They will have clean used clothes, from the top of their head to the bottom of their shoes. Before you start out, fellows, make damn sure to check each other out, not only to the clothes but also as to the identifications we gave to you.

HAWK: Any special time to get behind the fence?

LION: No, I would say around 10:30 but not later than 11:00. Prior to that time we will have someone park behind the fence, and when you drive up he will drive away and you park in his space. When you see the chief's auto on Houston, figure you have about seven minutes before he passes your spot.

BULLDOG: I wish we had a more accurate way.

EXECUTOR: Oh, but you will, you will. When the chief's car is at the corner of Houston and Elm, he will come to a complete stop. Now, when he starts to make his turn onto Elm, the other rifleman will count to five seconds and then start to shoot. You count three seconds after you hear the shots, and then you start firing.

BULLDOG: But this means we would have to look at our watches and this takes our eyes off the target.

Lion: No, Bulldog, you use the method used in track meets. You say to yourself, "1,001; 1,002; 1,003; 1,004," and so on until you reach 1007. That is seven seconds practically on the button.

HAWK: But that could make us shoot first, which we do not want to do.

LION: Hawk, you are missing the point. While you are saying those words, concentrate on hearing sounds like firecrackers. When you hear that, start at 1,002, and by the time you reach 1007 you shoot, shoot, shoot! We know how fast both of you are and we know your quickness and reactions tested on the firing range. If both of you were not good, you would not be here.

EXECUTOR: From actual tests we know that it will take a minimum of nine seconds to aim at your target and pull the trigger three times. This is not a "dry run," but aiming at a man whose head and body will be twisting and turning, waving at the crowd. And when that man is the chief of state, any rifleman is going to be under tremendous tension and pressure. No rifleman in the world can pull a trigger three times under those circumstances in less than nine seconds. Some horse's ass lawyer will probably set up some theory that it can be done, but he is not committing the murder.

BULLDOG: How many times do we fire? From what you have said we have to be finished and on our way in about thirty seconds.

EXECUTOR: That is correct, and that is why both of you and the other rifleman will be given only four bullets a piece. This will compel you to stop.

HAWK: What do we do after the shooting?

LION: First you make damn sure to pick up the cartridges. Since the station wagon is only fifteen to twenty feet away from the fence, simply take the rifles, get into the wagon, and drive away. The one who is not driving should put both rifles back into the golf bag and then put it under the floorboard.

HAWK: Where do we go?

EXECUTOR: Well, I see no reason why you should not enjoy a real hunting trip. So, drive up to our lodge and stay there a week or so and then come back here. Leave the wagon and everything else at the lodge. Someone will take care of it. By the way, both of you visit Dallas a week before the twenty-second, and make yourself familiar with the area. After that, it will be up to both of you. Well, that's all there is. Good luck and goodbye. (ALL SHAKE HANDS, and HAWK and BULLDOG depart through rear door.

EXECUTOR: (After a short wait.) Well, Lion, the bubbles will go out of the champagne on the twenty-second. It seems that everyone has a Rubicon to cross. Come, let us cross ours.

CURTAIN

End of Act II, Scene III.

Act III, Scene I: "Who Speaks for God? or Epilogue."

SOUND EFFECTS: When battlefield scene is being played, the background sound is taped. The sounds comprised jets and bomb explosions, including the whine of bombs in the air prior to striking the target. The sound of women and children crying or sobbing; appeals for help from the wounded on both sides; and napalm.

When the audience sees the casket in the church, the music is that of "Death March from Saul." Wail of the bagpipes and the role of the drums.

TIME: Past and present.

ACTORS: BATTLEFIELD CHAPLAIN, CHURCH CHAPLAIN.

CURTAIN

In this scene, Scene I of Act III, the stage is divided down the middle. On the left is the battlefield. On this battlefield are GIs who are attending church services. The pulpit is in the front of the stage. Further down is a group of GIs sitting on crates and, beyond them, the ground that was a battlefield; and on this battlefield are mannequin bodies dressed in Viet Cong garb. The service is actually held in a clearing surrounded by vegetation and trees, whose branches have been torn or shredded by shells. Bomb holes can also be seen. The glare from flame in the background is used to reveal the CHAPLAIN. The pulpit is actually a crate, over which has been draped a white cloth and upon it the cross.

The BATTLEFIELD CHAPLIN stands at an angle toward the GIs.

Stage right has the pulpit in the background, as in a church, and the CHAPLAIN speaks directly to the audience as he would in church. Thus, he would mount steps to be behind that pulpit.

In front of the pulpit a catafalque upon which rests a casket, which is draped with the American flag. A spotlight is used to light only the area of the casket. Another spotlight lights up the area surrounding the pulpit.

The lights on stage right go on first; then, after a few seconds, these go out completely; stage left is shown for a few seconds, and they then go out. The stage is dark.

Immediately, the lights go on over stage right. The music is muted as the church CHAPLAIN enters from front stage right, and proceeds toward the flag-draped casket, makes a bow, then turns and mounts the steps leading to the pulpit. As he lays down the Bible, which he has carried in his hands on the pulpit, that area of the stage darkens.

Stage left is now lit with battle flashes; sounds of war are muted. The BATTLEFIELD CHAPLAIN goes directly to the draped pulpit and begins:

CHAPLAIN: (After giving the sign of the cross to the soldiers.) Oh, Lord, our God, I summon your help for the mighty task you have imposed upon your soldiers. That task of crushing those who believe not in your words. We, who follow in your foot-steps, dedicate our lives and our souls for the eradication of those who refuse to accept your word.

May you give us strength to destroy those who would fail to bow to your commands. May we have the strength to use our weapons of flame to burn, to ground into dust the bodies of all those who refuse our command that they give unto thee their loyalty and devotion. May our weapons make the soil unfertile; the women to cease childbearing; the blood, bones, and sinews of the men ground into the dust as your punishment for their defiance of your holy command.

May you grant us strength to conquer in your name, and with that strength we shall put the fear of God in all the infidels on this part of the earth. In the name of Christ our Lord, amen.[24]

(The stage goes dark, then, after a few seconds, stage right is lit.)

---

[24] Cf. Mark Twain's satire on American imperialism, "The War Prayer" (ca. 1904-05): "O Lord our God, help us to tear their soldiers to bloody shreds with our shells; help us to cover their smiling fields with the pale forms of their patriot dead; help us to drown the thunder of the guns with the shrieks of their wounded, writhing in pain; help us to lay waste their humble homes with a hurricane of fire; help us to wring the hearts of their unoffending widows with unavailing grief; help us to turn them out roofless with little children to wander unfriended the wastes of their desolated land in rags and hunger and thirst, sports of the sun flames of summer and the icy winds of winter, broken in spirit, worn with travail, imploring Thee for the refuge of the grave and denied it – for our sakes who adore Thee, Lord, blast their hopes, blight their lives, protract their bitter pilgrimage, make heavy their steps, water their way with their tears, stain the white snow with the blood of their wounded feet! We ask it, in the spirit of love, of Him Who is the Source of Love, and Who is the ever-faithful refuge and friend of all that are sore beset and seek His aid with humble and contrite hearts. Amen."

CHAPLAIN: (In church.) Who bears the responsibility for the appearance of this flag-draped casket in this church? Why have we remained silent when we know that what was called good was, unto God's law, evil? Why have we tolerated the intolerant? Are we all not a part of the murder in Dallas? Have we not permitted the subversion of God's work to that of injustice?

Who shouts for war? Is it not always those who do no fighting? Is it not those the farthest away?

In the war raging today, the battlefield is over 7,000 miles away from our shores. Yet, it is we who seek the enemy in that far off, distant land. But do our youth go willingly?

The parents who cry out for war are the same ones who seek to protect their own. Today, we have reached the immoral, for parents now say let the other parents' son fight and die. Not theirs.

In this conflict, desired by no one, why is it that the old send forth the youth of this nation to die? For what purpose? So that the old may achieve immortality?

Is the uttering of the word "peace" such blasphemy that in the name of God we destroy the soul of man? Shall we entrust our living bodies and souls to those statesmen whose own sons refuse to fight on that battlefield? Where are those sons? Are they protected from shot and shell by hiding under an umbrella called the National Guard? Are they hiding under an umbrella called "the university"? How long will the disadvantaged die on behalf of the advantaged? Until God wills it? Or will they, in the near future, interpret "God's will"?

Who lies there, before us, a man or a nation? A nation conceived in liberty and dedicated to the proposition that all men are equal, or a nation whose conception of liberty has now degenerated into "might makes right"?

If we, as citizens of this great nation, permit the executioners of the man whose remains are closed within that casket to escape justice, we must then acknowledge the fact that we acquiesce in the murder. If we accept that proposal, then we have agreed that from this day forth human beings are to be used only as an instrument for the acquisition of power, regardless of the number slain in achieving that power.

The will of God can only be imposed by God himself. No man can proclaim to be God's instrument or have unto himself the right to act in God's name.

As long as we remain silent, we absorb the guilt. Blood may wash away, but the stain upon our conscience remains. God gave no right to no man or no nation to impose that man's or nation's theories upon others. God, in his infinite wisdom, proclaimed all men to be created in his image. Who are we to decide, on behalf of God, what color that image be?

Liberty can endure only as each man recognizes the liberty of the other. That concept that man remains free unto himself and to others, that liberty is a right and not a privilege, is a concept that sprung forth from great religious traditions. He who would chip away at liberty slowly places the chains around his own person. Freedom is more than a word, but those who only speak and never act deserve the chain they are about to receive. We bury the remains of a man in the casket, but shall we permit our leaders to use his shroud to conceal his murderers?

(Lights slowly dim out.)

CURTAIN

End of Act III, Scene I.

Act III, Scene II: "The Critique."

TIME: The Present.

PLACE: The Executive Office. Dallas, Texas.

ACTORS: KING, NOSLEN, PRINCE.

THE STAGE: The same as in Act I, with the following exceptions:

The rifles have been removed and replaced by bookshelves.

The animal heads have been removed and the space remains blank.

The Texas and Confederate flags have been removed.

All small Texas and Confederate flags have been removed.

THE PROPS: The entire Warren Report, twenty-six volumes and report, on bookshelves.

The U.S. code containing the McCarran Act, known as the "Concentration Act, USA," is on the bookshelf.

The book "Concentration Act, USA," is on the bookshelf.

A slide projector and slides.

A large silver screen, capable of receiving a six or eight foot picture. Screen must be movable, by hand or on wheels.

A large map of the Asian world, including all the islands.

A wooden pointer.

CURTAIN

PRINCE: Mr. King, have you heard the murmurings of the populace?

KING: Tell me what you have heard, and I will tell you if I've heard what you heard.

PRINCE: The gist of those rumors seems to be that the Commission knew that a conspiracy existed and that several federal agencies are involved.

NOSLEN: I've heard the same, and I admit I'm a little worried.

KING: Why worry? Both of you know that I have always maintained that nothing can or will touch us. As to the federal agencies, look how they are protecting each other. You know, Noslen, that there was dynamite in those Miami, Florida, police tape recordings. But what happened? Nothing, absolutely nothing.

PRINCE: That may be true, Mr. King, but what if the public forces the agencies to act? Then look at our position.

KING: Our position would still remain the same. Both federal agencies have informed the nation that nothing on those tapes pertain to the assassination. Do you think they are now going to admit the contrary? The three of us know that both of those agencies lied when they said that the dead chief had not announced his trip to Dallas. You and he (pointing to NOSLEN) and I know that the dead chief had announced his trip to Dallas to the Dallas press on September twenty-sixth. But both agencies, in their denial, did not point out that the informer gave that information to the Miami Police prior to the published announcement. Thus, both agencies have to protect each other.

NOSLEN: That may be true, but those agencies may then be compelled to give that evidence to our state authority. Then what?

KING: Nothing! The murder was a state crime committed in the state of Texas. Therefore, Texas will have to prosecute. So, the prosecution of the alleged murderers is right back here in the lap of our friends. We are not on those tapes. So I ask again, why worry?

NOSLEN: I'm not concerned about myself for the present, but how can seventy-five percent of the people be shut up?

KING: Well, Noslen, if we three know the truth that a conspiracy existed, why should not more than we three know the truth that the Commission's report is nothing more than 888 pages comprising a lie?

PRINCE: That is easy for you to say. However, if you had to work with the identical material that is in the report, the twenty-six volumes of the hearings, the reports issued by the SSB, the IIB, and the EIA, and the material in the National Archives, could you prove there was a conspiracy beyond a reasonable doubt?

KING: I could and would. I could do it right now within the confines of this room, within the next thirty to forty-five minutes.

NOSLEN: Now, that I refuse to believe. Are you telling me that there's legal proof published by the Commission or in the National Archives, or suppressed evidence of which you have knowledge, that proves a conspiracy? I don't believe it.

KING: Noslen, I will go further than making statements; I will put my money where my mouth is: say, an even stephen bet of $10,000.

NOSLEN: You're on! When do we start? Say, Prince, do you want a part?

PRINCE: Hell, no! If Mr. King says he can prove it, he will.

KING: Noslen, I'll even permit you to be the referee. I point out one thing to you, Noslen. Everything I will show you is available to every newspaper reporter and commentator.

KING: Prince, please bring the screen closer to the desk while I plug in this slide projector and get my private collection of slides.

(As PRINCE places the screen in the proper place on the stage, KING places the line into wall socket, unless the projector has its own batteries. KING then takes a key out of his pocket, unlocks dresser on left side of desk, and brings forth a box of slides which he places on desk. PRINCE and NOSLEN then stand to his left so as not to block view of audience. KING operates the slide while talking. The stage lights are dimmed sufficiently so that a perfect picture is cast on the large screen.)

KING: All right, gentleman, this is the first piece of evidence that led to the exposé of a conspiracy.

(KING inserts slide number one, which is a picture of the route published the morning of November 22, 1963 by *Dallas Morning News*.)

Now, Noslen, this is the only route map ever published in Dallas prior to or on the day of the killing. Notice, Noslen, that the map does not show any "double detour" but a route straight down Main Street.

NOSLEN: But that proves nothing.

KING: Oh, yes, it does. For then, the question is "Who guided the chief's automobile into a double detour which led the chief right past both ambush sites?"

PRINCE: Well, did the Dallas Police ever explain that detour?

KING: No, for the Commission never asked that question. So, Noslen, Patsy never knew the chief's route. Only those in the "know" gave the conspirators that information. (KING removes slide number one and inserts number two: USIA photo.)

This picture is link two of a conspiracy. This is the official combination photograph—diagram released by the USIA to the foreign press only. If you look closely, Prince, you can see why the photo was suppressed.

PRINCE: (Going near the screen.) Good Grief! The chief is definitely struck by two bullets and the governor by another one. Why, that's three bullets!

NOSLEN: That evidence is only a presumption. I want to know more than that to give you ten grand.

KING: Of course, you need more evidence. Here, take a look at this. (Inserts slide number three: the IIB report.)

(Caution to director: Under federal law, the words "Federal Bureau of Investigation" or "FBI" cannot be used in any stage, screen, TV, or radio play without written consent of the FBI. Therefore, always use initials IIB, which stands for "Internal Investigating Bureau." Thus, slide must use those words or initials, or face court.)

KING: This official report of the IIB was suppressed by the Commission. Notice, Noslen, that the bullet is a back wound, not a neck wound. In support of the IIB report is another suppressed document, but it can be found in the National Archives. (Here KING removes slide number two and inserts slide number four.)
   Well, Noslen, both bureaus support each other regarding the number of bullets fired. One bullet struck the chief, then another one hit the governor, and the third one hit the chief. Three bullets. Yes, Noslen, the Commission suppressed both reports. Why?

NOSLEN: Well, if I were on the jury, I would ask the same question. Counting the bullet which the Commission said was a total miss, plus those three bullets, it stands to reason that no rifleman could have gotten off four shots in the time specified by the Commission. But could those bullets have been fired from the sixth-floor depository window?

KING: No, they were not. I will prove that right now, with another suppressed photograph given to the Commission by the SBB. (KING removes slide number four and inserts slide number five.) This photograph, Noslen, is the official reconstruction of the location of the automobile when each man was hit by a bullet. Notice where the chief's automobile was when they were hit. It is a scientific impossibility for anyone firing a rifle from that sixth-floor window to hit either man in the automobile. (KING removes slide number five and inserts slide number six, which is a continuation of the SSB reconstruction. See National Archives.)

PRINCE: My God, this is incredible! I had no idea such photos existed.

KING: Neither did ninety-nine percent of the American people.

NOSLEN: Mr. King, did any other agency support the SSB reconstruction?

KING: Yes, Noslen, none other than the IIB, who said that the bullets that struck the chief in the back came in at an angle of fire between forty to sixty degrees. The bullets that struck the governor came in at a twenty-seven-degree angle. That, Noslen, proved that no bullets were ever discharged from that sixth-floor window.

NOSLEN: But the Commission's Report said that all the physicians testified to the fact that there was no back wound, just a neck wound. Who was lying?

KING: Not the doctors. There was a back wound and a throat wound, each caused by a separate and distinct bullet. Why, none other than the Commission's own medical witness testified two bullets were involved. Prince, go over to the bookshelves and pick out those two volumes. (PRINCE does so.) Open them up to page 365 and page 240. Read it. (PRINCE reads the sentences out loud.)

NOSLEN: I watched those TV programs relating to the Commission last year. They reaffirmed the Commission's report one hundred percent.

KING: (Heatedly.) Reaffirmed crap! Those TV reports were as phony as plastic baloney! To prove to you that there were two distinct bullets, here is the official autopsy chart called Commission Exhibit Number 387.[25] (Here KING removes slide number six and inserts slide number seven.) Well, Noslen, is that black dot a back wound or a neck wound?

NOSLEN: But the Commission's medical witness said that his pencil slipped when he made that dot.

KING: Slipped my foot! Here, look at the front of the body. (KING uses pointer.) Notice that there is a mark at the front of the throat and the use of the figures right next to the mark. Now, look at the back of the body again. (KING uses pointer.) There is no hole at the back of the neck. This means, gentleman, in forensic medicine, that the mark at the front of the throat is an

---

[25] Commission Exhibit Number 387 is contained in the *Warren Commission Report, Appendix 9*, "Autopsy Report and Supplemental Report," pp. 538-46.

entry wound. Forget about those TV programs. I'm discussing testimony given under oath.

PRINCE: Did any federal agency say there was a back wound?

KING: Hell, yes! Here is the official reconstruction of the location of where the bullet hit the chief.

(King removes slide number seven and inserts slide number eight. This is the IIB photograph showing location of wounds and back.)

Well, gentleman, is that a neck wound or a back wound?

PRINCE: You have convinced me it's a back wound. What about it, Noslen?

NOSLEN: I can only say that half of my bet is out the window.

PRINCE: In view of that, what was the official cause of death?

KING: The physicians at Parkland Hospital said death was the result of a massive wound over the left temple. Here, look at the autopsy report. (KING removes slide eight and inserts slide seven again.)

Notice the wound or mark over the left eye and on the right side on the back of the head. That is two bullets. Then another bullet in the back and still another one in the front of his throat. That, in my figuring, is four bullets. Now, Noslen, are you going to tell me that one bullet can travel up, down, right, and left?

NOSLEN: No, but since you have gone this far, what about the rifle, the palm print, and the hiding place? Certainly those elements must be taken into consideration.

KING: You are a hard man, Noslen, but for ten thousand you are entitled to the answers. Okay. Here is the official photograph of Patsy's hiding place. (KING inserts slide number nine.) See anything peculiar, Noslen?

NOSLEN: No.

PRINCE: (Laughing.) Boy, you're as blind as a bat! Hell, it's as plain as the nose on your face. Noslen, how the hell did Patsy get in and out of that hiding place? Look, it's at least six-feet high and closed at both ends. He couldn't get in; he couldn't get out!

NOSLEN: By God, you're right!

KING: Hooray, you are a commencing to use your head. Now, as to the rifle, here is an affidavit by the deputy sheriff who found it. (KING removes slide number nine and inserts number ten, featuring the Weitzman affidavit.)[26] This man, who had seven years experience in firearms, said it's a German Mauser.

---

[26] Deputy Sheriff Seymour Weitzman, who worked for the Dallas Police Department, initially identified the rifle as a 7.65 Mauser. Weitzman and Dallas Sheriff's Deputy Eugene Boone found the rifle "covered with boxes" inside the Texas School Book Depository. Weitzman later changed his testimony and claimed it was an Italian Mannlicher-Carcano.

NOSLEN: But, Mr. King, even an experienced rifleman can make a mistake?

KING: I grant you that, Noslen, but did a police captain and four other experienced policemen make the same mistake? Did the district attorney, who had that rifle in his possession for about eight hours, make the same mistake? In view of the fact that the D.A. was a former IIB agent for about six or seven years, did he make a mistake? Why, Mr. Noslen, the Commission admitted that the rifle they said was used to murder the chief had the words: "Made in Italy, 6.5 Caliber" stamped on the gun stock. Are you telling me that all these men, and the D.A., did not see those words when they inspected the rifle for identification marks? Come now, Noslen, let us not be stupid.

Noslen. No, I agree with you. But what about the IIB saying that Patsy used that Italian rifle?

KING: (Removes number ten, inserts slide eleven.) No, I'm sorry, Noslen, but you are one hundred percent wrong. The IIB simply said that Patsy OWNED owned an Italian rifle. They never said he USED it. There is a great difference between "owned" and "used."[27]

NOSLEN: Yes, I can read. I see the word and know the difference.

---

[27] The distinction between *owning* a weapon and *using* it to kill someone was raised by Leo Sauvage in his 1966 publication, *The Oswald Affair*, a book cited by Marks in the first MMF.

KING: I can give you some other vital information. The IIB never testified that the rifle they received from the Dallas Police was the identical rifle that the police say was found on the sixth floor. The only question that remains is how did the German Mauser become an Italian Carcano, and when and where were they switched?

PRINCE: Did you ever find out, Mr. King?

KING: No, I'm not interested. If you are, Prince, why not ask the police?

PRINCE: Stupid, I may be; crazy I'm not! Well, Noslen, can I take part of the bet?

NOSLEN: Go to hell! I know when I'm licked.

KING: No, no. Not yet. I am going to prove to you I'm one hundred percent right.

KING: Here, Noslen, is the front page of the Dallas newspaper published as the final edition after the murder. (KING removes slide number eleven and inserts slide number twelve: *Dallas Times–Herald*, final edition.) Notice that the first police broadcast was prior to 12:25 p.m. and not 12:30 p.m. Why do you think the Commission stressed that 12:30 was not the actual time, Noslen?

NOSLEN: How would I know? Is there any evidence to confirm the newspaper?

KING: The reason is due to the evidence that Patsy was talking to an employee between 12:15 and 12:25 p.m., when he then left the lunchroom to go outside on the steps to see the chief. This time of 12:25 was substantiated by another two sources, the *Morning News* and the actual police tapes, which revealed the receipt of the sheriff's statement at 12:26 p.m. So, the Commission, in an attempt to convict Patsy, simply moved the time forward.

(As KING makes a move to remove the slide number twelve:)

PRINCE: Wait a minute, there is something else that is important.

NOSLEN: What?

PRINCE: Look at that paragraph in the middle of the first column. Why, that says the shots came from the Dal-Tex Building. Let's see, it states that "the shots seem to come from the extension of Elm Street from just beyond the Texas Book Depository Building at the corner of Elm and Houston Street."

KING: I see that you are becoming interested, Mr. Prince. But do you also see how many men were arrested and where? Notice how many shots were heard? And where they came from? What happened to that evidence and those men, Noslen? What happened to the man arrested with a rifle in his hands in the Dal-Tex Building within ten minutes after the murder, Noslen? What happened to the man with the rifleman captured by the sheriff? Did the police test those rifles?

PRINCE: Jesus Christ! How many men did the cops arrest?

KING: Six that I did know of; as high as ten or eleven.

NOSLEN: If the Commission wanted to convict Patsy, then why did they involve him in the killing of the cop?

KING: Psychology or human nature. The more killings they placed upon Patsy, the greater the impact upon the public. That is why the Commission placed the attempt on that ex-general on Patsy's shoulder.

NOSLEN: Now, don't tell me that anyone can find evidence published by the Commission which proved Patsy innocent.

KING: (Laughing.) Noslen, do you want to throw away another ten grand or play double or nothing?

PRINCE: I'll take half of it, Noslen.

NOSLEN: Like hell you will! From the television and other newspaper reports published last year, there seems to be no doubt that Patsy was the only one involved in those affairs.

KING: Let me say that those reports were made by organizations who know on what side their bread is buttered. But if you want to listen for about five minutes, I can show you the facts behind those two affairs.

NOSLEN: Well, go ahead. This is the most expensive thirty minutes in my life.

KING: I'll get rid of the attempt on the ex-general first. The only witness to the attempt testified that two men, each driving an automobile, made the attempt on the ex-general's life. Patsy, as we all know, never drove an automobile in his life. So, that eliminated him.

PRINCE: Then what about the rifle? The IIB said it was used in that attempt.

KING: I wish you would go back to grammar school, Prince. The IIB never made that statement. In their official report to the Commission, the agency categorically stated that the rifle barrels may have been changed and that the slug taken from the ex-general's study could not be tested, because it was so mutilated.

NOSLEN: But the Commission said ...

KING: (Heatedly.) Screw the damn Commission! I am discussing law and evidence. There is no evidence, not a particle, that connected Patsy with that affair. Do you believe every damn thing you read?

PRINCE: I agree. So that leads us to the cop killing. It seemed to me that the television programs made a better case than the one against the chief. The TV reporters had the bullets and the witnesses.

KING: Like hell they did. They poured the largest pail of slop over the American public in the history of this country. How do you know, Prince, that the cop died from bullet wounds?

NOSLEN: Oh, come now, Mr. King, everyone knows the cop was shot three times.

KING: That's what you say. Can you prove it?

NOSLEN: You bet your sweet life I can. Just read the autopsy report.

KING: What autopsy report? The cop may have died from a heart attack, or TB, or overeating. There is no autopsy report printed by the Commission. I do know that there are four or five bodies from which the Dallas cops took various bullets. Based on that, I also know that no cop in the world has four or five bodies.

PRINCE: Where is this evidence?

KING: It cost me some money, but I had someone check into the files of the National Archives. There is a suppressed SSB There is a suppressed SSB [document that contains a report filed] by an agent of the SSB concerning the cop's death.

NOSLEN: Go on, what was in this report?

KING: It made my hair stand on end, and you both know it takes a lot to do that. However a police physician informed the agent that the cop was hit by four bullets, three of which penetrated the body and one glanced off.

NOSLEN: What's so strange about that?

KING: Damn it, wait a minute. I want to get this straight. However, the agent said three bullets hit the cop in the chest and one in the head. So, that makes it two bodies, is that not correct, Noslen?

NOSLEN: I agree. The doctor said his corpse had three bullet wounds. The agent now added a wound in the head for the fourth bullet. So, where are the other bodies?

KING: In the same report, the agent now stated that another policeman said the dead cop had a bullet wound in the stomach.

PRINCE: That's three bodies. Two more to go.

KING: Let me recollect. Oh, yes, the Dallas head of the SSB informed the Commission that the dead cop was hit in the head and twice in the chest. Now, this body is missing a bullet hole, for it has only two in the chest. The other agent said three in the chest. So, this makes four bodies.

NOSLEN: And the fifth?

KING: Well, a detective from the Dallas Police testified that the cop was hit once in hand, chest, and stomach. Now, we have a hand wound but no head wound. Five bodies, Noslen, five.

NOSLEN: (Laughing.) I do not want to believe it but I must. No wonder the Commission suppressed that document. How could a district attorney go to trial on that basis? An impartial judge would throw the case out of court.

KING: You are so right, Noslen. The judge would find Patsy not guilty, for there is no evidence as to the cause of death. Of course, there may be five bodies in the casket according to the SSB.

PRINCE: Mr. King, I understand that the bullets matched Patsy's revolver?

KING: What revolver? Bullets? What bullets? The IIB testified that the bullets they received from the Dallas Police were worthless. So that takes care of the bullets. As to the revolver, Patsy never had a revolver when he was arrested at the theater.

NOSLEN: Goddamn it! Mr. King, isn't anything the Commission printed the truth? What the hell, Patsy admitted he purchased the revolver.

KING: Don't you yell at me. If you would stop to use your brain, you would see that the revolver episode is identical to the rifle. Patsy purchased a revolver but he never used it. This is the IIB language being repeated. The bullets never matched his revolver.

NOSLEN: But what about the revolver that was taken from Patsy when he was arrested?

KING: Who said that the cops took a revolver from Patsy?

PRINCE: Why, the cops took it from him.

KING: Like hell they did. There was enough perjury by some cops to send a whole police force to prison. No cop who arrested Patsy ever testified that he took a revolver from Patsy. The cop who first said he took revolver from Patsy admitted to the Commission that he was wrong. He admitted that someone in the police station, after Patsy was charged with murder, gave him a revolver and said it was Patsy's. So, legally, there is not a gun, in view of the fact that two other cops admitted they never saw Patsy with a gun while being arrested.

NOSLEN: Christ almighty! You mean to say the gun evidence is a fake?

KING: Of course. That gun shown to the Commission was a plant. You tell me, Noslen, how Patsy's revolver could discharge a .38 automatic shell.

NOSLEN: It can't be done. Any cop or ballistics expert can tell you that.

PRINCE: My God, this is worse than *Alice in Wonderland*.

KING: No, more like Orwell's *1984*. The worst is yet to come.

NOSLEN: The worst? How could anything be worse than losing ten grand? Well, let me have it, for I'm paying for it.

KING: Within six hours after both murders the Dallas Police proved that a conspiracy existed and that some of the cops were involved.

NOSLEN: I know if I said "I don't believe it" you would chop my head off. So, let's have it.

KING: It is so simple that it is hard to digest. Here, both of you, look at this arrest sheet. (Now KING removes slide number twelve and inserts slide number thirteen, which is the Dallas Police Department charge sheet versus Lee Harvey Oswald.) Do you see anything of interest, Noslen?

NOSLEN: No, it looks like a simple charge sheet.

PRINCE: Noslen, you are wrong. Of course, you are not an attorney but I am. Patsy is charged with the murder of both the chief and the policeman at the time he was brought into the station. That was about half past two.

NOSLEN: So what?

KING: Well, two events occurred around 5:30 p.m. that day. One was a national television broadcast of a high executive official of the Dallas Police Department stating that the police had no witnesses to the man who fired the shots. The other one was another broadcast that Patsy had been arrested as the only suspect in the murder of both the chief and the cop. At 8:00 or 8:30 that same night another national TV chain broadcasted the fact that Patsy had been arrested for the murder of the chief. Now, Noslen, do you understand?

NOSLEN: No, I do not. What is so mysterious about those broadcasts?

KING: For Christ's sake, Noslen, wake up! How in the hell could the police charge Patsy with the murder of both the cop and the chief of state at 2:30 in the afternoon? Or even at 8:30 p.m.? This is why no one in Europe ever believed Patsy did it. For Christ's sake, even the police admitted they had no witness to identify the rifleman. Then how the hell did those arresting officers know to charge Patsy with the chief's murder? Who told them to file that murder charge? Look at the charge in the arrest sheet. It definitely states he killed both men and wounded the governor. How the hell did they know that before the IIB traced a mysterious rifle to Patsy? Why, Patsy's fingerprints or palm print were not even on that rifle. So, I ask you once more, Noslen, why did those cops file those charges?

NOSLEN: I can't answer that, but I concede you won the bet. However, may I ask a question?

KING: Go ahead.

NOSLEN: If you had not read the evidence, could you have found a conspiracy?

KING: Absolutely. I found evidence of the conspiracy by just reading the newspapers for three days after the murder.

NOSLEN: I don't believe it!

KING: Here we go again. Noslen, will you quit saying that. By now, you should know that when I make a statement I am speaking the truth. I'm going to show you the *New York Times* of November 23. (KING removes slide number thirteen and inserts slide number fourteen.) Now, you can read of two bullets. One bullet was to hit the chief of state over the left temple. Another bullet was in the front of the throat. Still another bullet hit him on the right side of the head.

PRINCE: But where is the back wound?

KING: Good point, Prince. Nothing is said of this bullet until the following day, and do not forget that the naval hospital did not release any autopsy report by its commander for three days.

NOSLEN: Yes, I would like to read that report; it would be interesting.

KING: *Grimm's Fairy Tales* are interesting reading also. There is no legal autopsy report and never has been.

PRINCE: No autopsy report? How can that be? Are you telling me that we have the same situation like that in the policeman's murder?

KING: You are not listening, Prince. I said there is no legal autopsy report. Legal, legal, legal. In another words, that autopsy report in the National Archives is a pack of lies, and there is no court in the United States that would permit it to be placed in the court record. As a legal document, it is a fake, a phony!

NOSLEN: I am not an attorney, but I'll bet that our citizens believe the doctors did make an autopsy report.

KING: Of course they do. Why shouldn't they? They are not lawyers, so they believe what they read. And the owners of the press didn't give a damn, and they still don't give a damn. In fact, I would venture a guess that ninety percent of them applauded his murder.

NOSLEN: Can you show actual proof that the autopsy report is illegal?

KING: Hell, that is the easiest thing to do. Here is the official exhibit of the alleged autopsy report. (KING removes slide number fourteen and inserts slide number fifteen.) Well, Prince, you are a high-priced attorney, and you have handled cases involving documents. Now, tell Noslen, is that a legal autopsy report?

PRINCE: (Going closer to the screen to see the picture.) No. Absolutely not. There are words crossed out, and this would vitiate the document unless the doctor who made the report could substantiate the original by the notes he made during the autopsy.

KING: No, the navy doctor admitted that he burnt all his original notes and then, Prince, he had the gall to admit, under oath, that his alleged report was based on a newspaper story.

NOSLEN: Hell, I don't have to be a doctor to know that is highly improper.

KING: Well, the Commission was not interested in the impropriety of the alleged autopsy report. Its sole function was to protect the murderers in the "interests of national security." As a matter of fact, the navy doctor admitted that there was a bullet wound in front of the throat. So, Noslen, there is your conspiracy. One bullet in the front of the throat, two in the head, and one in the back. The throat wound and the two head wounds were reported within two days after the event. That is how I know I could prove a conspiracy.

PRINCE: I understood that the Commission was referring to that famous bullet number 399. You know, the bullet they say was found on the stretcher.

KING: If you read the testimony in the hearings, you would find that if the bullet did not come from the back of the chief it could have only been a plant. If it was a plant, only two men could have planted it, either the Stripper or a member of the anti-Batista group of the EIA. Have you already forgotten that broadcast we heard from Great Britain telling about the fight outside the operating room? Every one of them carried a pistol, and any one of them could have planted that bullet.

NOSLEN: Did the police ever examine it to see if it corresponded to the Italian rifle?

KING: Of course not.

PRINCE: It has always seemed strange to me that the people swallowed that phony story about the bullet remaining in such shape.

KING: They should not be blamed, for the press never published this photo. (Removes slide number fifteen and inserts slide number sixteen: bullet dented.) This is the official photograph of a bullet when it strikes meat and bone structure. So, Noslen, do you still believe that the Commission were those truthful, honest, and loyal men you have spoken about so glowingly?

PRINCE: After listening to this absorbing tale of facts, I am a little overwhelmed. I have counted ten bullets fired at the chief of state, four of which struck him, and two bullets hit the governor. At least the Commission was consistent; it started and finished with lies.

KING: And one of those lies, my dear Prince, is the disappearing bullet! That is the only reason why the X-rays will not be revealed for seventy-five years.

PRINCE: That I do not understand. If you know, many others must also know.

KING: Of course other people know. If those X-rays are ever released, they will destroy the reputation of some of the highest persons in government.

NOSLEN: Well, so they are getting away with murder, but I say more power to them. Once those X-rays are released, we will also be finished. So, with no X-rays, no proof.

KING: Oh, how wrong you are, Mr. Noslen, how wrong you are! A person does not need those X-rays. I just proved to you, at a cost to you of ten grand, that a conspiracy did exist. I proved it, did I not?

NOSLEN: No, King, you missed the point. You proved it to me but not to the world. I agree that seventy-five years from now the truth will be out. But who in the hell will care when the pictures are released?

KING: You know, Mr. Noslen, the trouble with you and the majority of your fellow citizens is that you and they make up a nation of literate illiterates. You see and read but do not understand. Just like today. You saw and you listened but you never understood. I prove to you that those X-rays were not necessary, but you let it slip right past your nose.

NOSLEN: Well, damn it, what is it?

KING: The FOURTH bullet, you stupid jerk, the FOURTH bullet!

NOSLEN: What the frigging hell are you yelling about? What fourth bullet?

KING: You illiterate bastard. The bullet that went down into his lungs. It is still there! Now do you understand? Here, I will show it to you again. (KING now reinserts slide number fourteen in projector.)

NOSLEN: Oh, my God. My God! Of course, now I understand!

KING: Hooray! (Sarcastically.) Yes, Mr. Noslen, the fourth bullet. That is the only reason why the public cannot see those X-rays. The sensibilities of the dead chief's family have nothing to do with it. Those X-rays prove that two bullets hit him over the left temple and on the right side of the head; one in front of his throat; and one in the back, which did not go through his body but fell out and onto his stretcher.

NOSLEN: Is the bullet still in his body?

KING: Of course! The Parkland Hospital medical staff has never denied the fact that the bullet which struck the chief in the throat and coursed downward into his lungs was ever extracted. The alleged autopsy report of the Bethesda Naval Hospital does not show that this fourth bullet was ever extracted. In fact, the autopsy report, Exhibit Number 397, shows particles of the fourth bullet in his lung. So, Prince, since no doctor ever testified that he removed that fourth bullet, it must still be in the body.

NOSLEN: But, King, X-rays can deteriorate within five years. That time is nearly finished, and with it your proof vanishes.

KING: Well, before the proof vanishes, I am going to show you something that has only been shown to persons at the highest level of government. Here is an actual replica of the X-ray which shows the bullet in the lung, the fourth bullet. This proves the conspiracy.

(Show slide number fifteen.)

NOSLEN: I agree you have proved your case, King. But you have yet to prove your point to the general public. The actual X-ray cannot be shown.

KING: No, Mr. Noslen, the picture will vanish but not the physical evidence. That will last until the arrival of eternity.

NOSLEN: How is that?

KING: Open the casket, Mr. Noslen, open the casket and in it you will find the fourth bullet!

NOSLEN: One last question, King, if the investigation was reopened, could you prove a conspiracy and uncover the conspirators?

KING: Absolutely, Mr. Noslen. Of course, the new chief of state would have to give my Commission the identical power that was given to the former Commission. In fact, the whole damn conspiracy would be uncovered in less than two weeks; and, to top it off, I would only reexamine the original witnesses. The solution is right there.

NOSLEN: Well, here's my check.

KING: No you don't! Cash, Mr. Noslen, cash. Those frigging bastards in Washington have enough money to throw around.

Come on, let us go out and have lunch. I'll buy it. By the way, Mr. Noslen, do you think we will ever get out of Vietnam?

CURTAIN

End of Act III, Scene II.

Act III, Scene III: "Decay in the American Dream."

ACTORS: KING, NOSLEN, PRINCE.

STAGE: The same as in Scene II.

TIME: Same day, late afternoon.

CURTAIN: Opens with all three actors walking in from stage door, right. KING sits in his chair. NOSLEN and PRINCE sitting near him.

KING: Thank you, Mr. Noslen, for the excellent lunch and the money. Now, both of you want to know my ideas on the main accomplishment of the commission and how it affects world history. Right?

NOSLEN: Right. I cannot imagine the reason why the Commission permitted the publication of those twenty-six volumes. Without them, no one would have been able to uncover the conspiracy.

KING: The reason why those twenty-six volumes were published was due to the egotism of the lawyers who worked as aides to the Commission. They felt, some twenty-eight of them, that they had as much right to receive the plaudits of the citizenry as the seven commissioners.

PRINCE: But how could they fail to see that, once the evidence was published, they would open up a can of worms?

KING: You fail, Prince, to grasp the ego mentality of the legal profession. In my dealings with lawyers I have found many of them to have the soul of a pimp and the morals of a whore. The medical profession will soon be attaining that distinction also.

NOSLEN: That may or may not be true, but that does not explain the theory which led to the Commission's conclusions.

KING: That theory is easy to locate. It operated under a theory that those who could read, would not. Those who could see, would not see. Those who could investigate, would not. The Commission solely relied upon its reputation of its seven members to carry through its grand deception.

PRINCE: Have you drawn any philosophical conclusion from the manner in which the Commission drew its conclusions?

KING: The definitive conclusion that I draw is that any future chief of state can be murdered and his murderers remain unpunished on the theory that to discover them would be against the national interest – whatever the hell that means.

NOSLEN: After seeing you demolish the Commission's report, I agree.

KING: Of course, you should also realize that this new concept permits the formulation of forecasting the next assassination.

PRINCE: Oh, come on, Mr. King, that really is a far-out statement.

KING: No, it is not. In the future, if we elect a chief of state who has a philosophy diametrically opposed to that of the vice-chief of state, then the friends of the latter can murder the former under the guise that the chief is operating on a course inimical to their interpretation of what is best for the nation.

PRINCE: Who would commit and act like that?

KING: Why, you stupid son of a bitch! (Laughing.) What do you think we did?

NOSLEN: But that would imply that the vice-chief had a hand in the murder!

KING: No; you are not listening. I said friends of the vice-chief. After the deed has been committed he may then, and only then, receive information about his friends' involvement.

PRINCE: Then it becomes a matter of ethics. I would not like to be in his shoes.

KING: A real hot potato; for many of those friends have benefited upon his assumption as head of the nation. Look how many of them are in high government positions or hold valuable government contracts. So, what does he do?

NOSLEN: From a practical political standpoint, I would do nothing. Let time act as the softener of the deed. The public will forget.

KING: That is not the problem that must be faced in the future. For example, say the Elephant Party nominates the governor of New York and the governor of Khalif for chief and vice-chief in the forthcoming election. [28] Furthermore, say that both are elected for their respective position. Now enters the problem. How long will the governor of New York be permitted to live? The prospective vice-chief from Khalif despises education, housing, welfare, unions, teachers, professors, Medicare, Social Security, the poor, and the deformed. In fact, you name it, he hates it. But he loves war, as long as he or his family is not involved. In other words, a believer in Fascism, American style.

NOSLEN: I can only say that he believes in what we believe. As a matter of fact, we have already formed a group to support him, and we have a good chance to put him over.

KING: I noticed, Mr. Noslen, that you did not answer my question of how long will his chief be permitted to live?

NOSLEN: As long as he does nothing to interfere with our programs. The last one did and we stopped him dead.

PRINCE: Returning to more mundane things, I would like several answers. Was there any evidence to connect Patsy to the IID or EIA?

KING: Plenty. But first, what is an agent?

PRINCE: I would say anyone that accepts money from a federal agency.

---

[28] In 1967 rumors were afloat that Governor Nelson Rockefeller of New York would run for president, with Governor Ronald Reagan running as the vice presidential candidate. Reagan quashed the idea by flatly stating: "I am not interested in that proposal at all."

KING: No, that would be a professional informer, like the ones used by the IIB to convict a lot of innocent people.

NOSLEN: Well, the former head of the EIA said that a contract is the only method to convert a private citizen into that of an informer.[29]

KING: No. That statement was very clever, for that would absolve the Agency of all acts committed by their agents. I would say that any person who accepts the direction and control of his activity by the Agency is an agent. Money has nothing to do with it. Look how many persons volunteer for their activities.

PRINCE: Then Patsy was an agent for the EIA, and an IIB informer?

KING: Correct. Look at Patsy's record. He was ordered to learn the Russian language while he was a Marine. He was trained at a Japanese airfield as an agent. He was ordered to Russia as an agent while he was still in the Inactive Reserve and retained his Class A Marine security clearance. He returned and again acted his part as a Red and Bearded One sympathizer. He operated a one-man pro-Bearded One committee out of a room next door to an EIA-controlled agency. He was subject to arrest when he returned from Russia, yet no federal agency made the arrest. Why?

NOSLEN: But if Patsy was an agent, why have him killed?

---

[29] A reference to statements made by Allen Dulles while serving on the Commission.

KING: Why? Come off of it, Mr. Noslen. You were in this room when I gave the order to have him killed to prevent him from squealing. Don't act the innocent with me.

NOSLEN: Now, I suppose you are going to tell me that, if I read the evidence, we can find the killer.

KING: (Laughing.) I know it sounds silly, but you are so right. The Stripper only shot Patsy in the belly. A belly wound is not fatal if prompt medical attention is given.

NOSLEN: For Christ's sakes, isn't anything secret?

KING: Not in this case. For example, Mr. Noslen, about thirty minutes prior to the shooting, the Parkland Hospital medical staff was ordered to prepare the autopsy room for Patsy's body. Premonition, Mr. Noslen?

PRINCE: Mr. King, I noticed that you have been very lenient with the IIB and SSB.

KING: Regarding their investigations for the Commission there is no reason to attack them. I showed you more than twelve pieces of evidence submitted by them to the Commission that proved Patsy innocent. What more could they do? They never wrote the report. As to the EIA, that agency simply told the Commission to go to hell, and they did.

NOSLEN: But then, you are overlooking the Miami tapes and the telex message?

KING: No, I am not, for the Commission had the duty to investigate the conduct of the agencies, and I'm not interested in those matters at the present. The lack of guts by the Commission to undertake their own investigation of the agencies was not the fault of those departments.

NOSLEN: Outside of the Commission's conclusions, the strangest event was the conduct of the dead chief's brother. After all, he was the attorney general.

KING: I can clear up your bewilderment. We had him tied up in such a manner that he could do nothing. Actually it was very simple; for the new chief of state, under Executive Order Number 11130, effectively removed the brother from investigating or directing the activities of any agency involved in the investigation.

PRINCE: How was that done?

KING: Under the executive order, all federal agencies were directed to report, not to the brother, but only to the Commission. Hence, the agencies could do anything they damned well please, and they could report only what they desired to report. So, to attack the brother is highly unfair to him, for he had no power to act under the new chief's executive order.

NOSLEN: If that be the case, then we have nothing to fear, for any evidence that does not reach the public must be given to the state of Texas. Where would the public go if they did have new evidence?

KING: Nowhere, Mr. Noslen, nowhere. The public and the rest of the world will simply continue onto their merry way to hell.

NOSLEN: My, oh my, Mr. King, you are really pessimistic today. Nearly four years ago you said we were on top of the world. Today we are on our merry way to hell. Our position seems to be in reverse.

KING: Look around, Mr. Noslen. Do you see the hope that springs eternal?

NOSLEN: It all depends upon one's viewpoint, Mr. King. Our group, for all practical purposes, controls the world. Europe does as we command. South America jumps when we whisper. The Far East is our slave. Our military power is so great that no one dares challenge us. The world is our oyster, our Pax Americana! As for the Reds, they are isolated. If they move, they are dead!

KING: Mr. Noslen, at times you amaze me. If we move against those Moscow Reds we and they will lie in a common grave – if there be any survivors left to bury us.

PRINCE: Why, that sounds like peacenik talk. Better Red then dead!

KING: Prince, you're a horse's ass! The desire for peace makes no one a Red.

NOSLEN: Hey, cool it; cool it! Let us discuss this rationally.

KING: If my statement, Prince, is peacenik talk, then why is your son in college while another man's son is in Vietnam? Is it not true that your money keeps him in college, while the other man has no money?

PRINCE: Goddamn it! That is a low blow. What the hell, if you had the money, would you send your kid to college or to the battlefield?

KING: (Slapping desk.) Aha! Now we get down to the guts. Your patriotism is limited to your mouth. It is a question of life or death. You have no desire to see your seed destroyed in a civil war.

NOSLEN: For Christ's sake, King, if we do not stop them, they'll conquer everyone.

KING: As the paratroopers used to say, forty-six, forty-seven, forty-eight, forty-nine, same shit. Every imperialist power since the dawn of mankind has said the identical thing. And they used the identical words and the identical methods. They were bringing the blessings of civilization to the conquered people; and, by God, if those people refused to accept those blessings they were better off dead. By the board of the prophets, Mr. Noslen, we are going to make those damn "gooks" accept democracy if we have to kill the whole damn lot of them.

PRINCE: But we are different; we're civilized, not barbarians.

KING: How different? Do we have three of them instead of two? Are we so different that our instrument to procreate is different from theirs? In the eyes of God, Prince, who is different? Who is using napalm? Who used nuclear weapons? Did those barbarians in their history ever burn six million men, women, and children within a two-year period?

PRINCE: No, Mr. King, I disagree. Communism is barbaric and a danger to us. We want to use every weapon at our command to prevent that disease from engulfing this country. I say that we should fight it away from our shores; not on our shores. If those other people get in our way, that's too damn bad.

KING: If that be the case, Prince, then why fight it in Vietnam? I say that the only time we should fight on foreign soil is when the life of this nation is in danger; and only then should our citizens fight to uphold its existence.

NOSLEN: Why, that would soon …

KING: Let me finish! This nation's life is not in danger in Vietnam. No one threatens us; no one has invaded our native land. We have sold our honor and desecrated our ideals to fight a phrase called "communism." We are paying for that aberration in the blood, sweat, and tears of our less fortunate countrymen.

NOSLEN: But we must stop it; we must stamp it out whenever it raises its head.

KING: No, Mr. Noslen, you are completely wrong. I propound this question to you: If the brain, soul, and body of communism is in Moscow, why are we fighting it in Vietnam? Is it due to the fact that those Moscow Reds have sufficient nuclear weapons to destroy us as a nation? Do you honestly believe, Mr. Noslen, that if those Chinese Reds had about fifty percent of the nuclear weapons controlled by Moscow, that we would now be in Vietnam? Let us both be honest with each other. We both know the answer. Like hell we would!

PRINCE: But everyone knows Moscow directs all communist activity.

KING: You pain me deeply, Prince. I wish you would stop reading all the crap put out by your own propaganda machine. Communism is as monolithic as the Democratic and Republican parties in our country. Today, there are no monolithic unities. Look at Christianity. Who speaks for it? The Pope? How many types of Protestants exist in today's world? Nor have we any goddamn right to impose any sort of Christianity upon a Buddhist world. Hell, even the Jews, some of them, now eat bacon and eggs, barbecued ribs, shrimp, and anything else that tastes good to the palate. Why, I'm told they even mix *Fleishig* and *Milchig*!

NOSLEN: What the hell is that?

KING: (Laughing.) I really don't know. Something to do with not eating meat and milk at the same sitting. It's like asking the Orthodox, Conservative, and Reform Jew to pray in the same church. Instead of praying they have a royal battle. I guess they are just like us Protestants, when we disagree who will sit on the right side of God.

PRINCE: This information is all well and good. But I want to know how we can prevent communism from conquering us or the world.

KING: Democracy and communism are philosophical concepts of governing peoples and nations. If the philosophy of one type of government is repugnant to a nation, the people of that nation will reject it. To Asians, democracy is nothing more than a white man's method of controlling their lives. Those Asians will never accept democracy from the muzzle of a flamethrower or the stench of napalm burning the flesh of an Asian baby.

PRINCE: But those damn smaller "gook" nations will fall to the Reds. We must prevent that at all costs. Our honor is at stake.

KING: Prince, you are worse than a two-bit idiot. How are those Chinese or Moscow Reds going to conquer such nations as Japan, Australia, the Philippines, New Zealand, Okinawa, the Malaysian Peninsula, Formosa, Guam? How are those Reds going to reach Washington, Oregon, California, Anaheim, Azusa, and Cucamonga?

PRINCE: I don't know, but I feel it in my bones.

KING: I doubt if you have the capacity to feel a woman. How are the Reds going to reach those countries? By swimming? They have no fleet, no air power, and no economic base to support and equip the regiment, let alone an invasion army. Of course, Prince, they could use dragonflies.

PRINCE: Well, someone, some nation must stop this Red power expansion.

KING: You know, Prince, you are nothing more than a mealy-mouthed rabbit. No (raising hand), I apologize to the rabbit. At least he has some fun in life. You say "someone" or "some nation," but I ask you to interpret those two words. I am pretty damn sick and tired of listening to you and your kind always bleating about communism but only with your mouth. You want to use someone else's blood and guts to do the fighting, not your own.

PRINCE: You have two sons, and I notice they are still in college.

KING: And if I have anything to do with it, they'll stay there. Why should they fight? To defend whom? To defend what? You, your sons? The sons of newspaper publishers who are fighting this war on college campuses? The sons of congressional hawks who are carefully protected from active battlefield service? The men who have used the National Guard as an umbrella to protect themselves from the shot and shell of Vietnam? The sons of governors who accept money motorboat racing?[30] Prince, I ask you, how many sons of governors, senators, congressmen, state and federal judges, state and city legislatures are in Vietnam? Do you know?

PRINCE: How the hell do I know? Who can answer questions like that?

KING: Well, I can give you one answer. A survey of the 1964 Congress, which consisted of more than six hundred members, had exactly one son fighting in Vietnam. And I'll tell you something, Prince, when those sons of bitches send their sons to defend us on the battlefield, then, and only then, will I send mine.

NOSLEN: I admit that the attitude of the nation is different from 1941. But why?

KING: Why? For the simple damn reason that those congressmen and the others I named, including myself, fought everything Hitler and Tojo represented. But I'll be goddamned

---

[30] On November 26, 1967 Ronald Reagan's son Mike pocketed $7,700 for manning the helm of a motorboat during the last ninety minutes of a two-day race held in Arizona.

if those men and myself want our sons to die for some no good bastard who thinks that Hitler was the greatest man in the twentieth century. If we accept his hero, then we are spitting on the graves of nearly 400,000 Americans who died believing that America means more than a concentration camp. We would be admitting to ourselves that every one of them died in vain, and their death led not to man's liberty but to the creation of larger crematoriums.

NOSLEN: Since someone has to fight the Reds, the only problem is to find the answer to the question "Who?"

PRINCE: My attitude would be to let the poor white trash, the niggers, those welfare bastards, and the rest of them that don't like us.

KING: That is what I like about you, Prince. You have a highly consistent underdeveloped intellect. You are overlooking one essential.

PRINCE: What is that?

KING: You should know that, in today's armed forces, our soldiers and sailors are taught some highly intricate weapons. After we have trained them, what is to prevent them to turn on you? They will know how to use a tank, a machine gun, a flamethrower, and other weapons like antipersonnel mines and gas. Who do you turn to, Prince, when that happens?

PRINCE: Oh, we will organize some type of group like Hitler had, you know, his personal SS troops. With our money, we can buy anything.

KING: That is what I thought you would say. You are a consistent idiot. All right, Prince, say that we analyze the problem and do it by rational means. For the sake of discussion, Prince, let us assume that tomorrow you are the chief of state, and for your chief advisor you have that eminent Governor of Khalif, Governor Hameger. After all, both of you adhere to the same philosophy, and both of you proclaim your deep devotion to Christianity.

PRINCE: All right, I accept. I am the chief of state. Let us discuss the number-one problem, the Red conspiracy and involvement in Vietnam.

KING: By God, Prince, that is what I like about you. Persistent and consistent. Very well. The governor of Khalif's approach to Vietnam was to make a parking lot out of North Vietnam.[31] In other words, his Christian approach was the complete extermination of approximately eight million men, women, and children. From 1960 to the present, we have already killed more than one million souls based on the damage and death rained upon Germany and Japan in World War II. If we also include

---

[31] By the September 1967 California Governor Ronald Reagan was calling for an extreme escalation of the Vietnam War, to win it by whatever means necessary, using the military's "full technological power." In an October 10, 1965 interview with the *Fresno Bee* conducted during his California gubernatorial campaign he said: "It's silly talking about how many years we will have to spend in the jungles of Vietnam when we could pave the whole country and put parking stripes on it and still be home for Christmas." Stanley Marks rightly equates this with a policy of extermination. Reagan (here thinly disguised as "Governor Hameger") served as governor from January 1967 to January 1975. Even after he was elected president, Reagan never disavowed such radical views.

the number of unborn children to the men and women of North Vietnam, the ratio would be about another half million unborn children. Now, Prince, what happens?

PRINCE: Why, I would organize a new government. I would make a democracy. Of course, not a democracy immediately, but say within five or six years.

NOSLEN: How can you do that? If you have exterminated all of North Vietnam by using nuclear weapons, there is no one left to appreciate democracy.

PRINCE: Who said anything about nuclear weapons?

NOSLEN: Come off it, Prince. I know your views, and you have always harped on the fact that we should end the conflict quickly. Well, we've been in that hellhole since 1960 with all our conventional weapons and have yet to make them cry uncle. Don't start quibbling. You said you would accept the evidence of the Khalif governor, and he has publicly stated he wanted a parking lot. To me, that can only mean one thing, extermination.

KING: I agree with Mr. Noslen's reasoning. The North Vietnam are all dead, and you have used their blood, bones, and muscles to mix with the cement that made the parking lot. Now, what do you use it for?

PRINCE: I'd go right up to the Chinese borders, put in atomic installations, and tell them to stop their aggression against their neighbors. If they fail to agree, I'd go to war.

KING: The Chinese Reds tell us to go to hell. Do we, I mean, do you, attack?

PRINCE: Absolutely. I would use every weapon in our arsenal, from nuclear weapons to gas. To me, the only good Red is a dead one.

KING: I agree with you, Prince, that we would win. Now, you have physically destroyed some eight-hundred million Chinese and conquered all of the Asian mainland. What will the Russians do? Will the Moscow Reds permit you to construct airfields one-hundred yards from their Siberian borders? Will they permit you to construct naval bases at the northernmost point of China?

NOSLEN: I believe, King, that the Reds would surrender if we gave them an ultimatum. Surrender to us, or they die. They know that we have a nuclear superiority of more than four to one. They know that we have in excess of seven thousand nuclear warheads in Western Europe. I am of the firm belief that the Russian people would overthrow the government and the communist system if they knew that we would seriously be willing to go to war to destroy communism. After all, deep down, the Russians are a God-fearing people, and they know that God is on our side.

KING: I'm happy to know that God is on our side. I do wonder, however, if he will turn aside all those Red nuclear missiles when they let them go at us. Is the angel Gabriel going to catch those missiles on the fly as they go past his pearly gates on the way toward us?

PRINCE: Now, do not become sarcastic, Mr. King. This is a serious matter.

KING: But I am serious, very serious. Prince, you have always stated your views that the Reds, of any stripe, are paranoiac. Insane people who should be put to death. Well, if the Reds are insane and paranoiac, then I would submit to you that those Chinese Reds, once attacked, are going to let loose with the twenty to thirty hydrogen bombs they now possess.

NOSLEN: That may be true, but they can hit only a limited number of targets. They do not have any long-range delivery system. Of course, they can destroy the Philippines, all of Japan, Okinawa, Malaysia, and parts of India. But those people are only "gooks."

KING: So democracy marches on! Well, Prince, you have now decimated ninety percent of the yellow race, and we two-hundred million white American Christians control a dead Asia. But what about those damn Reds? There are some 225 million. Do we still kill them all, Prince? What happens, Prince, if those damn Reds fight back? What happens to us?

PRINCE: Nothing. Oh, we may lose eight or nine million, but that is about all. We have been very fortunate in our wars. Today, we have four of the greatest fleets ever assembled in civilization. The Reds have no fleet that can either destroy those four fleets or mount an invasion.

KING: Would it surprise you, both of you, that those Russians need less than sixty hydrogen bombs to destroy us as a national unity? Sixty hydrogen bombs, wrapped in cobalt or sodium, is less than ten percent of all their hydrogen bomb arsenal in their ICBM inventory.

NOSLEN: You say ten percent? Sixty bombs would destroy us? That's a stupid statement.

KING: Not stupid; only honest. Our Defense Department has admitted that the Reds have in excess of six hundred ICBMs capable of hitting any target in our country. I am not exaggerating if I believe that ten percent of them will strike the target; that is, a major city or industrial complex. Do you agree, Mr. Noslen?

NOSLEN: I do not question your statement.

KING: To continue. Those Red missiles have the strength of a twenty-megaton explosion. If this missile was exploded at three thousand feet, the effect would destroy every living person in a thirty-mile area. At twelve thousand feet, the blast would destroy lives and property in a one-hundred-mile radius.

PRINCE: Would the Reds strike at civilization or military targets?

KING: What the hell is the difference? This is total war. What do you think we are doing in Vietnam? Employing some native to run ahead of our planes, warning the people to seek shelter?

NOSLEN: We dropped leaflets to warn them.

KING: Hurrah for our side! And you know that less than fifteen percent of the Vietnamese read. That is really applying salvo to our conscience!

PRINCE: Well, what targets do the Reds hit?

KING: The best, Prince, only the best. New York, Philadelphia, Boston, and the Washington–Baltimore area. Four bombs for each target city, which would use only sixteen hydrogen bombs tipped with cobalt or sodium. With their combined explosion, about thirty-five million Americans die.

PRINCE: But that's inhuman!

KING: Why inhuman? Is not the use of napalm or antipersonnel bombs dropped indiscriminately inhuman? Are you contending that the men whose skins are not white are not made in the image of God? Since when has God segregated his images? I have never read that in the Bible. However, I am digressing. At the same time the Reds fire those sixteen hydrogen missiles, they also fire three bombs each at Chicago, Detroit, Pittsburgh, and Cleveland. Let's see, sixteen and twelve is twenty-eight, which still leaves those Reds with thirty-two hydrogen missiles.

NOSLEN: You are making the next war look simple and easy.

KING: Of course World War III is going to be quick, but many deaths will not be easy. I continue. Since the Reds are paranoiac, they also fire two hydrogen missiles at Omaha, Memphis, St. Louis, Cincinnati, Twin Cities, and Denver. That is only a total of forty missiles.

PRINCE: You seemed to have wiped out everything above the Mason-Dixon line.

KING: No, I'm saving that for the last. Let me see. Oh, yes. I forgot your advisor. The Reds would certainly enjoy leaving him with a greeting card. So, one missile, with love, for Sacramento, and one each for Los Angeles, San Francisco,

San Diego, Portland, and Seattle. Now, the Reds still have fourteen left. With those fourteen, the Reds would eliminate Dallas, Houston, Birmingham, New Orleans, Pensacola, and Atlanta. That leaves the Reds with six bombs to play around with.

PRINCE: And pray tell, who gets those?

KING: Oh, three bombs for the Great Lakes and three for the mountain ranges.

NOSLEN: Why there?

KING: That is the source of our water supply. Contaminate water, and people die within eight or nine days. No water, no life. Do not forget, those bombs are using cobalt and sodium material. So, Prince, with a lousy sixty bombs, those paranoiac Reds have wiped us out as a nation.

NOSLEN: But, my God, the Reds would also be wiped out. What would that accomplish?

KING: You stupid son of a bitch, the same thing you advocate. "Better dead than Red," only in the reverse: better dead than American.

NOSLEN: The only thing I can say, Prince, is that you certainly picked a lulu for your advisor.

PRINCE: Don't underrate him. He may one day become our chief of state.[32]

KING: Well, I have never overestimated the intelligence of our people. They have been swallowing the crap on TV for the past four years, so they will probably swallow him.

NOSLEN: But where will it all end? Do you now regret our act of '63? Would history have been any different if we had not acted?

KING: Different? Yes, but whether it would have been good or bad, I can give no answer. I know something is missing: a vision, a spirit. All I know and feel is that the nation is not using all eight cylinders. The nation's foundation seems to be crumbling.

PRINCE: I certainly agree with you Mr. King. Why, I've given thousands to various groups who want to shore up the foundation. Just look at our schools, the damn Supreme Court, the lousy hippies that walk the street, those goddamn draft dodgers, labor unions. Why, even the damn teachers want to drive Caddies! What the hell is this country coming to? Everyone wants to enjoy life. Damn fools; for them, there is no such thing.

KING: Prince, you are the right side of a horse's ass; the left side I leave to the Commies; and the center I give to your advisor and his friends. And you do know what the center is, I hope?

---

[32] The author's prediction that the "Khalif" governor, Ronald Reagan, would one day become president came true a dozen years later, when Reagan was elected as the fortieth president of the U.S.

NOSLEN: Philosophically, what is the difference between '63 and '68, Mr. King?

KING: I would say the difference expressed in the "Star-Spangled Banner" and "America the Beautiful." One is a war hymn; the other, peace. Today, "Bombs bursting in air" must mean nuclear bombs. If that occurs, Mr. Noslen, who will remain alive to enjoy "America the Beautiful"? Furthermore, how can America be beautiful if the landscape is dotted with concentration camps?

PRINCE: Wait a minute! You mean camps like Hitler's?

KING: Yes, like Hitler's. Don't you know anything about the Concentration Camp Law enacted by our liberty loving liberal Congress in 1950?

PRINCE: I never heard of it. You must be pulling my leg.

KING: No, I am not. Mr. Noslen, please bring the U.S. Code from the bookshelf.

(NOSLEN goes to bookshelf, removes Code, and walks back to King's desk, where he lays the book down.)

Open up the Code to the McCarran Act, Title 2, Section 100, and tell our friends.

NOSLEN: (NOSLEN reads to himself.) By God, he's right! Jesus Christ! I would not believe it myself if it wasn't before my eyes. Let's see. The 1950 Internal Security act, sponsored by Senator McCarran of Nevada. Supported by Hubert Humphrey, Paul Douglas, Harley Kilgore, Scott Lucas, John F. Kennedy,

Richard M. Nixon, etc. Only seven senators voted to support a vote of "Give 'em Hell Truman." Hmmm. Hmmm.

PRINCE: Stop mumbling. What does it say?

NOSLEN: The law stipulates that the chief of state has the right, at any time, without the consent of the Congress, to declare an internal national emergency. Once he does that, the chief of state can arrest and imprison any person who he thinks will probably engage or probably conspire with others in acts of espionage or sabotage.

PRINCE: But there must be some standard before he can invoke the law.

NOSLEN: Oh, there is, but the chief of state has tremendous leeway. If Congress declares war, he can invoke the law. If there is an invasion of the United States or its possession; or if there is an insurrection in the United States.

PRINCE: I can understand the declaration of war, but what about that language "an invasion of our possession or an insurrection." Hell, under that law, if the Japanese rioted on Okinawa, the chief of state could invoke the law here in this country. That island is under our possession and comes under the interpretation of the act.

KING: But what about an insurrection? Didn't your friend, the Khalif governor, say that the student disturbances on the campuses were, in his words, "insurrections"? Would you trust him with this kind of law? What about the peace marches? They are against authority. Under our English common law, they could be considered insurrections. And what about strike violence? You would like that, you and your friend, the governor.

PRINCE: Jesus Christ! That would mean that anyone can accuse anyone else of acting against the government and he can be put in a camp. That is essentially what the people of Germany did under Hitler. But what about a trial by jury or before a judge?

NOSLEN: No, Prince, the way this law reads, there is no trial, no hearing, no judge, and no appeal. The accused is picked up by any police agency, in any town, village, city, state, or federal land, and transported to a concentration camp.

KING: For your information, Prince, the Language of the McCarran Concentration Camp Law is identical in effect with Article 1 of the order of Protective Custody enacted by Hitler and his party in February 1933.[33] The only difference is that our law is in English. The Nazi law was printed in the record of the Nuremberg war trials of 1946. So, Prince, our liberty loving American congressmen and senators had four years to study the Nazi law and decided Nazism was good for us.

---

[33] Civil liberties were effectively annulled in Nazi Germany by the Presidential Emergency Decree of February 28, 1933, which empowered the Gestapo to imprison perceived "enemies" of the state (e.g., Jews, political dissidents, and other persecuted minorities) without any due process and any minus any judicial proceeding. In the Orwellian lingo of the Nazis this was termed "protective custody." (Also referred to as Article 1 of the Decree of the Reich President for the Protection of People and State.)

NOSLEN: I think, King, if you look back to the time when this law was enacted that the country was in the throes of a Red Scare.

KING: What a lot of crap! Every time any government desires to restrain its citizens it always has the excuse that it is being threatened. This is how man's freedom has been reduced throughout the ages. If that is the case, Mr. Noslen, then tell me why that Concentration Camp Law is still on the books? Who is threatening the citizenry today? This law is nothing more than the granting of weapons to police forces to extort and blackmail throughout the country. We are aping Hitler to the nth degree.

PRINCE: But our countrymen will not permit concentration camps. We're civilized; we're religious. Our Christian upbringing will not permit it.

KING: Where have I heard that before? The Germans were civilized until they adopted Nazism. You forget, Prince, that too many people practice Christianity only between 11 and 12:00 a.m. on Sundays. Show me a parishioner who is always proclaiming his Christianity, and I will show you a man who is not. As an old German philosopher once said: "Man is but an ape in velvet clothes."[34]

---

[34] In his book *The Two Christs* Marks refers to the German saying, "Man is but an ape dressed in velvet." Other collections of German proverbs reproduce it as "Apes remain apes, though you clothe them in velvet." And a British variant renders it: "An Ape is an ape, though clad in purple."

PRINCE: I don't care a hoot and a holler about Nazism, but I still maintain no one in our country will accept Nazism or its practices.

KING: Prince, I will prove to you, by your own logic, that you and your kind will accept the practice. Are you game?

PRINCE: All right, go ahead and I'll listen.

KING: You say that you believe in law and order? (PRINCE nods "yes.") The Concentration Camp Act is the law of the land, and it should be obeyed. Correct? (PRINCE nods "yes.") Under this act, the chief of state is the only one who can determine an "insurrection," and, once he determines that, he can invoke the act. Am I stating this correctly, Prince? (PRINCE nods "yes.")

NOSLEN: One moment please. What is an insurrection? A group of college kids making a "panty raid"? Some kids in Harlem or Watts throwing bricks at passing automobiles? Those women marching in Washington to petition Congress for peace? Motorcycle gangs raising hell in a small town? What is an insurrection; that is the gimmick.

PRINCE: That would have to be answered by the chief of state. I assume he could limit his proclamation to a specific area.

NOSLEN: I have just read you the law, Prince, and there is no such thing. It is applicable only on a nationwide scale.

PRINCE: Well, then, a court of law would have to decide.

NOSLEN: What the hell are you talking about? There is no provision for any court, state or national, that can interfere. You are refusing to face up to the fact that the Concentration Camp Law is nothing more than the final step to a dictatorship in this nation.

KING: Face up to the music, Prince. Now, what do we do with those three million Americans arrested under that law? Where do we put them?

PRINCE: What three million? Where did you obtain that figure?

KING: I'm surprised at you. You know as well as I that the IIB has a list named Operation Dragnet, which contains the names of every citizen whom the IIB considers a Red. Why, back in 1950, the head of that bureau testified that he could imprison 555,000 citizens under the Concentration Camp Law. This is 1968, and if you consider the Bureau's request for funds under that law, the minimum number is in excess of three million.

NOSLEN: But that cannot be correct. He must be confusing Reds with liberals.

KING: No, to him everyone who makes a left turn is a Red.

PRINCE: My God, where does he obtain his evidence? Under Hitler, any person who had one-eighth part of Jewish blood in him was a Jew. According to the Bureau chief, anyone who has ever talked to anyone who thinks he is a Red is considered a Red. And don't forget, his files go back to 1924.[35]

---

[35] In 1924 J. Edgar Hoover was appointed director of the Bureau of Investigation. In 1935 its name was changed to the Federal Bureau of Investigation (FBI). Hoover's directorship there continued until his death in 1972.

NOSLEN: Where does he obtain the names? How does he keep them under observation?

KING: The obtaining of names is very simple. The IIB analyzed the Gestapo methods and refined them. Of course, the IIB has more sophisticated equipment, like the UNIVAC 1108,[36] which it purchased for two and a half million dollars. This UNIVAC can store the names of more than ten million persons; and, if the Bureau decides to locate them, the UNIVAC can produce a name within twenty seconds.

PRINCE: The chief of the IIB had to have some standard. What was it?

KING: The Bureau has the name of every person who ever signed any type of petition since 1924. This includes the two million names on the peace petition sent to Stockholm; the names who signed for the Henry A. Wallace third party;[37] the Ban the Bomb petitions; the more recent Peace and Freedom Party. The Bureau even has the subscribers to all the liberal magazines extending back to 1932. As the Gestapo did, so does the Bureau; for if the mother or father signed anything from 1924 on, the names of the children are also placed on the list. Don't forget, Franklin D. Roosevelt, his wife, and his family were labeled as "Reds" by the IIB chief.

---

[36] A 36-bit computer system produced in 1965 by Sperry Rand.
[37] Wallace served as thirty-third vice president of the United States (1941-45, under FDR), and he ran for president under the Progressive Party ticket in the 1948 election.

PRINCE: All right, so he has three million names, but that is a long way from placing them in concentration camps.

KING: How wrong you are, Prince! We have inactive concentration camps in New York, Florida, Arizona, Oklahoma, California, Alaska, and Washington. Congress has appropriated millions in the past seven years, under the aegis of the Bureau of Prisons, to create another fifteen camps. The original camps can handle about 125,000 inmates.

NOSLEN: I do not believe that the IIB or the chief of state would place any of their political opponents on the list. It would be too damn obvious.

KING: It would be obvious, that I will grant you. But who would do the protesting? As a matter of fact, the IIB has admitted that they have already printed one million federal internal security emergency warrants. Many of those warrants have the names of the person to be eliminated.

PRINCE: Do you know anyone on the list?

KING: Of course I know. There are four Supreme Court justices on the list, fifteen federal senators, some thirty-five congressmen, about twenty-five federal judges, and a smattering of city mayors and state governors. Naturally, any person who has ever opposed the chief of the IIB is on the list and will disappear the day the emergency is effected.

NOSLEN: (Sarcastically.) What did you do, mail a letter to someone and ask for the list?

KING: How did you guess? You are absolutely right. Anyone can write to the U.S. Government Printing Office and obtain the records of the HUAC,[38] which list the names of persons who are allegedly Reds. You buy the list for each session of Congress. So, you now have a proscribed list dating back to 1933. Another book you can purchase is used by the Madison Avenue gutless ad agencies. On the local level, write to the Un-American Committee of the state legislature, and they will give you their list of names. For example, Mr. Noslen, in the state of Khalif, they have a one-man committee who has more than 250,000 names on his list, dating back to 1932.

PRINCE: So, there are a lot of names on a lot of lists. What can that Khalif one-man committee do?

KING: Under the Concentration Camp Law, the chief of state, or his delegate, or the delegate of the delegate, simply supplied the Khalif one-man committee with 200,000 to 300,000 blank emergency warrants. This one man inserts the name, and he turns it over to any police agent or even a special agent. The same person is secretly arrested and quietly shipped to one of the twenty-four concentration camps. Now, Mr. Noslen, do you see what a beautiful instrument for extortion and blackmail

---

[38] The House Committee on Un-American Activities (HCUA), also known as the House Un-American Activities Committee (HUAC). Stanley would have been well aware of HUAC "blacklists," because he was among those that were blacklisted. In the *Investigation of Un-American Propaganda Activities in the United States*, App. Part IX (U.S. Government Printing Office, 1944), his name appears on pages 296, 297, and 303. And in the *Fourth Report of the Senate Fact-Finding Committee On Un-American Activities: Communist Front Organizations* (The California Senate, Sacramento, CA, 1948), Stanley is listed on p. 95.

those warrants become? As in the Gestapo, thousands of our fellow citizens are going to become rich overnight.

NOSLEN: Have you ever seen one of those warrants, or are you fabricating it?

KING: In a case like this I never fabricate, Mr. Noslen. For your edification, here is a sample of the detention order. (KING takes out slide and inserts it into the projector.) I will also show you some forms that have the names on them.

(KING flashes on the screen the following names: Robert Kennedy, Edward Kennedy, Jacob Javits, Eugene McCarthy, Fulbright, Abe Fortis, Thurgood Marshall, Mark Hatfield, Young, Ralph Yarborough, Wayne Morse, Ernest Gruening.)[39]

---

[39] Senator Edward Kennedy of Massachusetts, brother of John and Robert Kennedy, who successfully sponsored over three hundred bills. Jacob Javits, liberal Republican senator of New York who supported labor unions and civil rights, and who opposed U.S. involvement in the Vietnam War. Eugene McCarthy, Democratic Party presidential candidate in 1968 who ran on an anti-Vietnam War platform. Democratic Senator J. William Fulbright of Arkansas, who opposed American involvement in Vietnam and supported détente with the Soviet Union. Abe Fortas, appointed by President Truman to delegations that helped to organize the U.N. As an associate justice of the Supreme Court he pushed to extend due process rights to legal minors and to transform the juvenile justice system. Thurgood Marshall, civil rights lawyer who fought against racial segregation in schools and who later served as the first African American justice of the Supreme Court. Republican Senator Mark Hatfield of Oregon, an early opponent of U.S. involvement in Vietnam, who also supported the Civil Rights Act of 1968. Democratic Senator Ralph Yarborough of Texas, who supported racial integration in schools and who voted in favor of the Civil Rights Acts of 1957, 1960, 1964, and 1968; the

Of course, Noslen, you realize that I could stand here for the next two weeks and keep flashing their names. But those are the main ones.

PRINCE: Now, Mr. King, I know you are making it all up. Those men cannot be arrested, since they are federal congress-men and senators. Under the Constitution they are not subject to arrest.

KING: Go back to law school, you chump! The Constitution only says that they are not subject to arrest while Congress is in session. Once the session is completed, their immunity vanishes. And believe me, they will vanish between the Capital and their homes, without a trace.

NOSLEN: I find this fascinating. Imagine, in this day and age, a federal Congress writing its own death warrant. All the gods must be laughing until they cry. Incredible!

24th Amendment to the U.S. Constitution (banning the poll tax as a prerequisite for voting); and the Voting Rights Act of 1965. He was the only Confederate-state senator to vote for all these bills as well as for the confirmation of Thurgood Marshall to the Supreme Court. Senator Wayne Morse of Oregon, who was one of only two senators to oppose the Gulf of Tonkin Resolution, which authorized President Johnson to bomb North Vietnam without a declaration of war. Ernest Gruening, a Democrat representing Alaska, was the other senator who voted against the Gulf of Tonkin Resolution. "Young" may be Andrew Young, an early leader in the civil rights movement and the executive director of the Southern Christian Leadership Conference, who was with Martin Luther King when King was killed in 1968.

PRINCE: What I find incredible is the fact that, if you know these facts, then those legislators must also know them. Why do they permit the law to exist; why not revoke that law?

KING: For the reason that they are godless. Who fought the law initially? None other than the so-called reactionary senators. Men like Langer, Mundt, Ferguson, every one of them a reactionary. Yet every one of them denounced that law as the Concentration Camp Law. And only ten senators fought to uphold the vote. In fact, Langer died on the floor of the Senate fighting this law. And where were the liberals? Fighting like hell to get the law enacted. So much for liberals. When the chips were down, they faded in the stretch.

PRINCE: But that was more than eighteen years ago. Where are they today?

KING: Prince, be a realist. Today, what can they do? Who controls the House and Senate? We do. Look at the chairmen of the vital committees in both Houses. Every single one of them is under our control. Who controls the police power of this country? Look at who is in command of the Department of Justice, the army, the navy, the Defense Department. Who controls the IIB if not a man who believes in what we believe? Who controls the EIA if not a fellow Texan? My God, do you also want to control heaven?

PRINCE: I don't give a damn who controls this country. I maintain that our countrymen are not barbarians. They will not permit those camps.

KING: You know Prince, you are an ignorant person.

PRINCE: Now, just a minute. My failure to agree with you is not ignorance.

KING: Oh, how right you are. There is a difference between ignorance and stupidity. Prince, you're stupid! You said that, in your opinion, the only good communist is a dead one. Am I correct?

PRINCE: Yes.

KING: Okay. Then let us proceed to the next step. You say that the law should always be obeyed. Morality has nothing to do with the law. Correct? (PRINCE nods "yes.")

KING: This McCarran Act, or, as I call it, the Concentration Camp Law, is now the law of the land. Now, Prince, so that we understand each other: this law gives the right to the chief of state to call a state of insurrection and then arrest persons he thinks will commit acts inimical to the nation. Correct? (PRINCE nods "yes.")
   Now, Prince, would you agree that you would accept the word of the chief of the IIB, the SSB, the EIA, the Armed Forces Intelligence Service, and the federal and various state Un-American Activities Committees[40] that, if they say a person is a Red, he is a Red and should be placed in a concentration camp?

PRINCE: Yes, I would agree with that statement. Those members are one hundred percent Americans and very efficient Red hunters.

---

[40] The remark about HUAC "state committees" may be an oblique reference to Stanley's own blacklisting in California, mentioned in the previous note.

KING: I admire your devotion to American ideals, Prince. Now, to the next step. Prince, you and the Khalif governor are members of the same political party. The emblem is the elephant, which is an animal that has an undersized brain and an oversized ass. All of you are always whining about taxes and balancing the budget. So, Prince, I ask you, from the concentration camp area is not the next step the crematorium?

NOSLEN: I cannot follow your reasoning.

KING: My reasoning, I assure you, Mr. Noslen, is a straight line. It will take tax money to feed and house those two- to three million concentration camp inmates. After a period of five or six months, the governor of Khalif will start crying that the way to reduce taxes is to eliminate the people in the camps, since food costs money. So, Prince, since the only good Red is a dead one, the next logical step of yours and of the governor would be to feed them to the furnace. Of course, to repay for that food, your friends will first extract the gold from their teeth and make sure not to break their glasses.

PRINCE: (In anger.) You son of a bitch; son of a bitch! That is not my philosophy. What American is going to shovel other Americans into a furnace? We are a highly Christian nation. We do not do things like that!

KING: (In anger.) Don't you raise your voice to me. You stupid prick! Who put people in the furnaces in Germany? Who were the camp guards? Who took the gold? Who sold the glasses? Who committed the tortures? Who put Polish Catholic nuns into Nazi troop whorehouses? Who burned those churches in Europe while the people were still praying to Christ? Who,

Prince, who but none other than your one hundred percent white Christian German?

PRINCE: But we Americans do not have that kind of upbringing.

KING: Don't try and crap me, Prince. Hell, the IIB already has a list for of men for camp guards. Who is blowing up those churches and synagogues? Who is throwing dynamite in the black schoolrooms? Who uses tear gas that blinds the peace marches? Who tortured and butchered those civil rights workers? Who is going around the country saying "The only good nigger is a dead nigger"? And who believes him, Prince? Why, none other than your goddamned one hundred percent white Christian so-called American. So, don't crap me that we are better than they. And you wonder why the youth of today refused to believe in that type of god!

NOSLEN: From your passion it seems to me that you believe that there is not much worth saving in the country.

KING: Mr. Noslen, how much lower can we sink? The American Dream is becoming a nightmare. Look around you and what do you see? A chief of state who says "You all can dissent, but keep your damn mouths shut." A Congress who has given dictatorial powers to the chief executive. A Congress that keeps the Nazi Concentration Camp Law as the law of the land. Look around and what else do you see? Now we have letter openers, wiretappers, and concentration camps, all legal.

PRINCE: But wiretapping is used only to check on criminals.

KING: It went right past your nose, Prince. Who are criminals? Under the McCarran Concentration Camp Law one man has the exclusive power to declare any man a criminal. And he can do this without a trial, a jury, or a judge. For all I know, Prince, you may be a criminal; and I, also, may be one. But only if you harm the state. That is a statement that can only be made by a communist or a fascist. Who decides whether or not I have harmed the state? You, my next-door neighbor, my enemy, or someone who tried to extort money from me by threatening to denounce me to some American committee? Or by wiretapping my telephone or the bedroom when I make love to my wife?

PRINCE: How can wiretapping lead to the concentration camp, King?

KING: Wiretapping, my dear friend, is the start of a triple play.

NOSLEN: Triple play?

KING: Yes, from wiretapping,

PRINCE: This is a depressing outlook. You give the nation no hope.

KING: Oh, but I do, I do. Like in Dickens' "Scrooge," I have attempted to show to you the past, present, and future. We have permitted the deed to lead us toward the future. A nation without vision can never progress toward the future.

Look around, Prince, and what vision does our generation reveal to our young? Just pick up any newspaper. Crooked politicians, bribe givers and bribe takers; wiretapping; mail-letter openers; wife swapping; lawyers and doctors who violate their own code of ethics and who protect each other;

businessman who sell contaminated food by paying off underpaid food inspectors; automobile manufacturers who deliberately sell death-dealing products; army and military officers who have retired wealthy. Those are what our kids see as the vision.

NOSLEN: But those are the exceptions – a few bad apples.

KING: No, Mr. Noslen, it is not a question of a few bad apples. What our youngsters see is the refusal to remove those bad apples from the barrel. We permit those few bad apples to contaminate the entire lot.

Those kids out there are too sophisticated not to understand the inequities of the method in which the draft law is wrong. Why do you think that the governor of Khalif has fought for a large increase in his university fees? To cover costs? That's a lot of crap, and you know it, I know it, and those kids know it; it is nothing more than a method of pushing the poor kids into Vietnam. The poor go to war, the rich go to college.

Face up to it, Mr. Noslen. Our generation made a mess of it. We set the example, and when the kids follow our example we bitch like hell. By God, if I were in my twenties, I'd be a hippie; at least they are trying to live their lives without using napalm or nuclear weapons. Four-legged animals protect their young; the two-legged ones compel their young to die for the benefit of the old.

I say that when liberty is forbidden, then extremism used to obtain that liberty is a virtue; and he who uses extremism is defending the right given to him by God.

Well, it is late and I'm tired.

(KING rises as do NOSLEN and PRINCE. KING walks to right front stage door, opens it, and turns toward them.

KING: I know of your plan, Mr. Noslen. I hope you plan well.

NOSLEN: Sir, I studied under a master.

(KING goes through door, leaving it open. PRINCE starts to say something but NOSLEN puts his fingers on his own lips. As the footsteps recede, shots are heard, lights dim, and a WOMAN'S VOICE cries out:)

WOMAN'S VOICE: My God, my God, they've killed him, they've killed him!"

CURTAIN

On the Life and Times of Stanley J. Marks, by Rob Couteau

"Rats have their feast wherever they choose – but they
shouldn't eat the pigeon in his nest."

"The heart of history … holds us by the throat, no more and no
less." – From the wartime anti-Fascist texts of Pablo Picasso.

I suspect that few JFK assassination researchers have led as interesting and diversified a life as Stanley Marks, whose Zelig-like appearance at certain key moments in twentieth-century history lends his biography an eerie and remarkable flavor. Born in 1914 in Waukegan, Illinois, when he was just four years old Marks lost both his parents to the ravages of the 1918 influenza pandemic, which infected a third of the world's population (from January 1918 to April 1920). He was eventually cared for by Sarah and Samuel Markowitz, foster parents who lived in Chicago. Mr. Markowitz worked as a tinsmith in a Russian-Jewish ghetto, and it was from him that Stanley took his surname. Stanley later shortened it to "Marks," hoping in this way to avoid the prevalent anti-Semitism that created obstacles to employment. His actual name remains unknown. According to his daughter, Roberta, Stanley never had enough food to eat while he was growing up on the hardscrabble city streets; and in the extant photos of him from this period he appears as a rail-thin young man. One can easily imagine how this subsistence lifestyle influenced his decision to become a lifelong "New Deal" Democrat.

Waukegan was host to a military base, and by the fall of 1918 it was one of the most dangerous place to reside in Illinois; for the mass mobilization of military personnel during World War I was a principal factor in spreading the deadly disease. It remains uncertain whether it originated in Europe or, as contemporary research now suggests, in Kansas; but as soldiers shipped out and returned to port cities such as Waukegan it rapidly jumped from naval bases to the civilian population.[41]

Waukegan had the misfortune of being home to the Great Lakes Naval Training Station – ground zero of the first infections in the state. A quarantine was established for 1,000 of the 50,000 men on the base, but visitors were allowed to come and go, which led to the spread of the illness to Chicago, only forty-seven miles south of Waukegan.

On September 16, 1918 the *Chicago Daily Tribune* featured a story about the arrival of the influenza in the Windy City, yet health officials continued to tell citizens not to worry. This lackadaisical approach helped to fuel the explosion of the pandemic. All too late, the health department recommended the use of gauze masks, which were termed "sneeze guards" or "germ screens." By mid-November there were 37,921 influenza cases;

---

[41] See John M. Barry, "The site of origin of the 1918 influenza pandemic and its public health implications," *Journal of Translational Medicine*, January 20, 2004, ncbi.nlm.nih.gov. According to Barry's research, Haskell County, Kansas may have been the influenza epicenter, with the outbreak dating from around January 1918. From Haskell it spread to Funsten, Kansas: the very place where Army personnel from all around the county were required to report for training. "Friends and family visited them at Funston. Soldiers came home on leave, then returned to Funston.... On March 4 the first soldier at the camp reported ill with influenza at sick call. The camp held an average of 56,222 troops. Within three weeks more than eleven hundred others were sick enough to require hospitalization, and thousands more – the precise number was not recorded – needed treatment at infirmaries scattered around the base."

13,109 cases of pneumonia; and a combined mortality rate of 51,030. Poor immigrants such as those living in the Markowitz neighborhood were hit the hardest. By the end of the Great Influenza Pandemic in the spring of 1920 there were between fifty million to one-hundred million deaths, with a death toll in the U.S. of 675,000.

Although Stanley's foster family was registered in Chicago's U.S. Federal Census for 1920 and 1930, Stanley's name does not appear in any of these households. His whereabouts remain unknown until 1932, when he enrolled at the University of Chicago. (This according to newspaper articles about him that were published in the early 1940s.) Two years later, he graduated from the University of Illinois at Chicago with a major in history. On August 1, 1936, about four months after his twenty-second birthday, he married Ethel M. Milgrom, a native of Chicago.

The following year Stanley graduated from John Marshall Law School, which is still Chicago's only public law school. According to the university's yearbook, he was a member of the Debater's Forum, a group composed of students, faculty, and alumni whose debates (on "important topics of the day") were broadcast every Saturday night over Chicago radio station WJJD. Such events paved the way for his later guest appearances as a political commentator on the CBS radio station, which occurred in the late Thirties or early Forties. Besides featuring a photo of his participation in a university debate, the yearbook lists Stanley's occupation as that of a "Salesman."

Why was a law school graduate working in sales? According to Roberta Marks, her father had a natural proclivity and passion for this profession, but there may have been another reason that he chose this line of work. The Great Depression of 1929 had reached a peak of devastation in March 1933, when a quarter of the work force – about fifteen and a half million –

were left unemployed. That year Stanley was completing his first year as a freshman undergraduate. After he finished his graduate studies in 1937, the Depression would continue to wreak havoc until at least 1939, leaving plenty of lawyers without work.

According to a 1940 federal census, Stanley and Ethel were living with Ethel's parents in an apartment in North Monticello Avenue in Chicago. Ethel's father, an immigrant from Poland, owned and operated a laundry, where he labored an average of seventy-three hours a week. Ethel's mother, a Russian immigrant, assisted him while raising Ethel's younger sister. The Milgroms also owned a grocery store in a predominantly Black neighborhood, where they extended credit to customers and developed a reputation for being very well liked and respected by their clientele. Stanley's lifelong devotion to civil rights may have been influenced by the Milgroms' respect for the African American community.

By now Stanley was employed as a salesman for the Illinois Vending Company. He would soon become a sales rep and personnel manager for Gardner and Company, a large firm that manufactured billboards and sales boards. But what the census fails to mention is that by 1939, while working full-time at his day job, he was also conducting research for a book about Soviet Russia. And somehow he received assistance from President Roosevelt's Secretary of State, Cordell Hull, who granted this young author direct access to State Department files. Hull was the longest-serving Secretary of State in U.S. history, and in 1945 he received a Nobel Prize for his role in establishing the UN. Since Stanley was helping to write publicity for the Democratic National Committee, his work with the DNC may have provided him with some sort of contact with Hull. He also relied upon his own personal library for research: a collection of about 5,000 volumes, mostly on military and political subjects.

In September 1942 Stanley signed a publishing contract with Dorrance and Company for *The Bear That Walks Like a Man: A Diplomatic and Military Analysis of Soviet Russia*. Released in February 1943 – a few months before his twenty-ninth birthday – this 340-page tome became a bestseller and received glowing reviews in over thirty mainstream papers. He later told a reporter that he worked on the project "four or five hours a night, five nights a week ... for three and a half years," and that the profits enabled him to purchase "a nice home."

By the end of March *The Bear* came to the attention of the *Chicago Tribune*, which featured a lengthy review titled "A Recital of Russia's List of Grievances." The author was a highly esteemed gentleman named John Cudahy: a Harvard graduate and World War I veteran who had fought with the American Infantry against the Bolsheviks in Russia's Civil War. Cudahy later served as FDR's ambassador to Poland and Belgium, and as minister to Luxembourg and the Irish Free State. By 1941 he'd published a half dozen books, and that same year *Life* magazine commissioned him to interview Hitler. Cudahy commended Stanley's book for its "detailed recitation of Soviet past grievances against the Democratic Powers – all the more painful for being irrefutably true."

What makes Stanley's accomplishment even more remarkable is that his publisher, Dorrance and Company, was a vanity press. Yet his publishing contract stipulates that Dorrance would pay for the printing of the book (highly unusual for a vanity press), and it offered the author a standard royalty payment. His only financial obligation was to pay for publicity in periodicals of his own choice. Gordon Dorrance, a former editor with Scribner's who'd founded the company in 1920, was later portrayed on the *I Love Lucy Show* in an episode called "Lucy Writes a Novel."

The spring of 1943 proved to be a watershed moment for the young author. After receiving so many positive reviews for his first book, Marks then pursued a teaching career at the Abraham Lincoln School for Social Science, which opened in Chicago that same spring. Founded by the Black civil rights activist William Patterson, this innovative, progressive institution was geared toward "workers, writers, and their sympathizers" (in Patterson's own words); and it assisted Blacks who were migrating from the South, hoping to find work in Chicago's factories. It was supported by "liberal educators and philanthropists" and "business people who supported New Deal liberalism."[42] Artists and writers such as Rockwell Kent, Howard Fast, and Paul Robeson lent their support; and Chicago-based literary authors such as Nelson Algren and Richard Wright were invited to lecture there. The school was one of the first to offer a jazz history course (taught by the Black activist and journalist Frank Marshall Davis), and it arranged for lectures to be held in factories where its students were employed. But due to the ramping up of the Cold War and the shifting political tides of post-WWII America, the school was forced to shut down after only three years. All the while, the institution remained under the surveillance of J. Edgar Hoover's FBI, particularly since Patterson was a member of the American Communist Party and had been arrested for protesting the execution of Sacco and Vanzetti.

By the end of April 1943 Stanley was also working as a book reviewer for the *Chicago Defender*, a widely celebrated paper for Black Americans. Thanks to its founder, Robert Abbott, in 1918

---

[42] Ian Rocksborough-Smith, *Black Public History in Chicago: Civil Rights Activism from World War II into the Cold War*, Champaign, IL: University of Illinois Press, 2018, pp. 31-40.

the *Defender* played a pivotal role in encouraging Blacks to leave the South and join a "Great Migration" to the North. On May 1, 1943 (International Workers' Day), the paper announced a new weekly feature: "War and Warfare: A New Column on Military Strategy and Tactics" by Stanley J. Marks. Each edition of the paper published both a book review and an essay by Stanley, whose tenure with the *Defender* continued through July 3, 1943.

During the Second World War the *Defender* supported the efforts of other Black newspapers to promote a "Double Victory Campaign": a dual victory over both foreign *and* domestic "enemies" who remained opposed to racial equality and justice for all. The movement grew out of a "letter to the editor" written by James Thompson of Wichita, titled: "Should I Sacrifice to Live 'Half American?'" Published in the *Pittsburgh Courier* on January 31, 1942, Thompson's words touched a chord, and a "Double V Campaign" rapidly blossomed across Black America. Double V baseball games, "victory gardens," and dances were organized by Black communities; and Double V clubs staged protests, met with Congressmen, organized bon voyage parties for soldiers shipping off, and pressured businesses to halt discriminatory hiring practices. As a result FBI Director Hoover – who considered such acts to be "treasonous" – almost convinced President Roosevelt to prosecute Black press leaders under the Sedition Act. [43] Although Hoover was ultimately forced to end his plan to censor and imprison the editors, this didn't stop him from continuing to spy on the Black press, as the FBI files attest to.

---

[43] According to author Patrick Washburn, Hoover prepared "a lengthy wartime report" on African Americans, twenty-five pages of which "dealt with Black papers." See Patrick Washburn, *The African American Newspaper*, Northwestern University Press, 2006, p. xvii.

How quickly political tides may change – along with the shifting currents of personal fortune. Even while the USSR remained our ally during World War II the oligarchy was already planning for an imminent Cold War. In 1944 the U.S. Government Printing Office used taxpayer dollars to publish a Bible-thick tome with a diabolical title: *Investigation of Un-American Propaganda Activities in the United States.* Stanley had the honor of appearing on three separate pages.[44] His thought crimes include working as an instructor for the progressive Abraham Lincoln School; composing "articles for labor papers"; and "having written favorably about the Soviet Union" (since *The Bear* highlights the role played by our Soviet ally during World War II: a nation that sacrificed millions of lives in the war against Hitler). He also made the grave error of writing about antilabor campaigns launched by politicians in the U.S. (e.g., "The new Congress is greatly reactionary due to the combination of Southern Democrats and Northern Republicans whose record of antilabor and antiprogressive laws needs no repetition here").[45] The House Un-American Activities Committee report (HUAC) also includes an entire chapter on the Abraham Lincoln School for Social Science, noting that it "makes a special effort to cater to members of trade unions."[46]

The groundwork of HUAC's investigation of the school was neatly prepared by an exposé published in the October 12, 1943

---

[44] *Investigation of Un-American Propaganda Activities in the United States, App. Part IX pages 261-1048*, U.S. Government Printing Office, 1944. Marks is cited on pp. 296, 297, and 303.

[45] *The Bear That Walks Like a Man: A Diplomatic and Military Analysis of Soviet Russia,* Dorrance and Company, 1943, pp. 277-78.

[46] *Investigation of Un-American Propaganda Activities in the United States, App. Part IX pages 261-1048*, pp. 292-309.

edition of the *Chicago Tribune*. Under a glaring banner headline, "Red Teachers on Faculty of Lincoln School," a reporter breathlessly intones that the institution "represents one of the most ambitious attempts yet made by the internationalists allied with advocates of communism to train a large corps of expert propagandists to further their attacks against the American republic."[47] How ironic that the same paper that had hosted John Cudahy's exuberant review of Stanley's text just seven months earlier now referred to him as the "author of the radical book, 'The Bear That Walks Like a Man.'"

Marks was inducted into the Army at Fort Sheridan, Illinois on March 1, 1945 and was assigned to the Tank Destroyer Replacement Training Center at Camp Hood, Texas. It didn't take long for him to garner some publicity. On April 12 six articles about Private Stanley J. Marks appeared in Sunday papers published in Camp Hood, Fort Worth, Victoria, Kilgore, Taylor, and Llano, Texas. Most of the headlines playfully imply that Stanley knows more about the history of military science than do his superiors: "Colonels Don't Tell This Private Much," "Army Private is Army Authority," "This Rookie 'Knows it All'." The articles also note that since 1943 Marks had been working on a 750-page "History of the U.S. Army and Military Science" (which features chapters on the "military arms and tactics of other nations as well as the United States, and sections on sea power, logistics, and military administration"). By this time the Army must have decided to commission Stanley to complete the work, because one article reports "the War Department has given permission to print it as a whole after the war."

---

[47] "Red Teachers on Faculty of Lincoln School," *Chicago Tribune*, October 12, 1943, pp. 1, 12.

The fact that a "blacklisted" soldier would receive glowing reviews and be the subject of sympathetic human interests stories serves as an example of how conflicting forces within the Establishment were playing themselves out during this time. While the military welcomed leftist veterans from the Abraham Lincoln Brigades who had fought against Franco in Spain, J. Edgar Hoover remained deeply suspicious of them and demanded that they not be promoted through the military ranks. A *Fort-Worth Star Telegram* article ("Army Writer at Camp Hood") even casually mentions the fact that Marks had taught at the Abraham Lincoln School: the very institution the Cold Warriors had labeled as a "Commie front" and that led to Stanley's public condemnation.

Marks' personal life mirrors in microcosm what was happening across a broader political spectrum. He was caught in a vise between the liberal FDR guard and an increasingly powerful right wing, the latter embodied by the likes of the Dulles brothers, J. Edgar Hoover, Joe McCarthy, and the Eisenhower–Nixon clique. Although he was blacklisted in 1944, Marks may have continued to benefit from his contacts within the Democratic Party throughout 1945. Thus, his status in the military may have seemed secure. After all, how many Army privates establish contacts with figures such as Secretary Hull or receive such positive media attention despite having been slandered by HUAC?

By the summer of 1945 Stanley was stationed in the Philippines and serving under General MacArthur, Supreme Commander of the Southwest Pacific Area. According to Roberta, her father was placed in charge of a publicity office, where he wrote and edited a staff newspaper. By the end of the year he served under Major Forrest Kimmerle, Commander of the U.S.S. Funston, who wrote Stanley a letter of commendation praising his morale-boosting work as editor of the ship's daily newspaper.

Stanley was honorably discharged in 1946. Two years later the California Legislature published its *Fourth Report of the Senate Fact-Finding Committee On Un-American Activities* in which Stanley's name again appears, this time in a section titled "Communist Front Organizations." Under a subsection, "Abraham Lincoln School," we read: "This Communist institution was established in the early part of 1943 ... as a streamlined version of the Workers' School which was openly run by the Communist Party [...] Among those with Communist or Communist fellow-traveling records connected with the Abraham Lincoln School are the following ..." Stanley's name is listed here, along with thirty-three others.[48] This same HUAC report features nine pages on author Dalton Trumbo's "Communist" record. (A screenwriter and the author of a popular 1939 antiwar novel, *Johnny Got His Gun*, Trumbo was one of the "Hollywood Ten" who refused to testify before HUAC.) During this period Ronald Reagan, then president of the Screen Actors Guild, was secretly cooperating with the FBI as an informant, handing over names of actors that he deemed to be "Communist sympathizers." (Reagan's code name was "T-10.") By 1948 HUAC's Hollywood hearings were in full swing and generating plenty of publicity. As Marilyn Monroe's husband, the playwright Arthur Miller, later remarked: what better way to get front-page headlines than to talk about "Commie" movie-star celebrities?

Back in 1944 *The Bear That Walks Like a Man* had also received an upbeat review in *Billboard*, a widely circulated entertainment

---

[48] *Fourth Report of the Senate Fact-Finding Committee On Un-American Activities: Communist Front Organizations*, The California Senate, Sacramento, CA, 1948, p. 95.

and music industry magazine, which is still being published today. But with the inception of an increasingly chilly Cold War, *Billboard* would soon be singing a different tune. In September 1950 it featured an article linking the Abraham Lincoln School to the Red Scare. Titled "Subversive Groups–Duck 'Em"[49] it includes the Abraham Lincoln School in a list of organizations that "appeared to be adjuncts of the Communist Party." By now, the FBI was monitoring the school and its staff, and the National Security Agency (NSA) also had an eye on the institution. In a June 3, 1953 NSA memorandum, "Affiliation or Association with Organizations Having Interests in Conflict with Those of the United States," the Abraham Lincoln School is sandwiched between a listing of the Abraham Lincoln Brigade and the Action Committee to Free Spain Now.[50]

It still remains unclear how Stanley's blacklisting may have affected his personal or professional life. According to Roberta Marks it wasn't something that was ever discussed at home, and until I conducted my research she had no idea that her father had ever been blacklisted or that his name had appeared in such reports.

On the one hand it seems odd that this otherwise prolific author – who would publish at least twenty-five books in his lifetime – almost completely vanishes from the public record during the years of the Red Scare. On the other hand, when he

---

[49] "Subversive Groups–Duck 'Em," *The Billboard: The World's Foremost Amusement Weekly*, September 2, 1950, pp. 5, 11.

[50] NSA Memorandum Number 120-26: "Affiliation or Association with Organizations Having Interests in Conflict with Those of the United States," dated June 3, 1953 and accessed in May 2020 at the Internet Archive. It's possible that the Abraham Lincoln School was associated with the Abraham Lincoln Brigades, which had fought the good fight against Franco's dictatorship in Spain.

was discharged from the Army in 1946 at the age of thirty-two, he was the father of a five-year-old daughter and had a family to support; so his energies may have been focused on earning a living and relying on his skill as a salesman. Roberta added that her father was a highly regarded business consultant who received many contracts to restructure sales departments of major companies, an occupation that he pursued throughout his lifetime. He was also engaged in various entrepreneurial ventures of his own. (For example, in the early Fifties, he formed Shower Enclosures Inc., which sold doors for bathroom showers.)

Shortly before her twenty-first birthday Roberta moved to LA to seek her fortune in the art-and-design field, since there were few opportunities in Chicago. Her father visited her during a business trip a few weeks after President's Kennedy's assassination, and Roberta still recalls his reaction: "He was very depressed. We were all depressed. It was such a traumatic time. There was an overall heaviness and gloom. Everyone was heartbroken; it was devastating. And anyone who was a *normal* person would be depressed! Like most people, I think my father felt that the election of Kennedy was like a breath of fresh air. Someone younger, to move the country forward. My impression is that he was totally enchanted by JFK." It was also a challenging period because Stanley was looking for work and attempting to gain a foothold in LA in order to remain close to Roberta.

The following year Roberta's parents relocated to LA; and in early October Stanley formed a new business corporation, Interstate Sales Counselors Ltd. While working full-time five days a week as a consultant, on evenings and weekends he began to compose what would prove to be his most innovative work on the JFK assassination: *Murder Most Foul! The Conspiracy That Murdered President Kennedy: 975 Questions & Answers.*

Published under his own imprint (The Bureau of International Affairs), it was released in hard cover and in paperback in September 1967. According to various ads that appeared in the *Los Angeles Free Press* (a popular counterculture newspaper), besides being sold in local bookshops orders were processed and shipped directly from his home on North Laurel Avenue.

Although Marks would never again receive the high-profile recognition that was generated by his first book, the publication of *Murder Most Foul!* did not go unnoticed. Ever aware of the need for publicity – especially for a self-published title – on the inside cover of the paperback he reproduced reviewers' blurbs from ten periodicals, including *Police Journal*, *West German Press*, *Midwest Book Syndicate*, *Law Journal*, *Pacific Coast Book Review*, *India Press Summation*, *Northeast Review*, *Naval Quarterly*, and *Marine 'Scope*. And somehow, he also managed to get *Murder Most Foul!* mentioned in a mainstream paper. A journalist with the *San Francisco Examiner* includes a brief mention of the title in a December 24, 1967 column, "Donald Stanley on Books – New and Notable": "A Los Angeles attorney and author gets in on the Kennedy assassination furors with a paperback listing of 975 questions and answers." Even in 1967, getting a self-published book mentioned in mainstream media could not have been easy.

What makes *Murder Most Foul!* such an exceptional text for its time? As Jim DiEugenio has noted in his 2020 essay, "The Dylan / Kennedy Sensation,"[51] four major cornerstones set it apart from the work of contemporaneous researchers.

First and foremost, the author's "political views on the

---

[51] James DiEugenio, "The Dylan / Kennedy Sensation," March 30, 2020, Kennedys and King website.

assassination, especially those at the end, are far ahead of the intellectual arguments in classic texts such as *Accessories After the Fact* and *Six Seconds in Dallas*, both published in 1967." To cite one example, consider Q&A #46 from *Murder Most Foul!*: "What is meant by 'against the national interest'? The Warren Commission has never defined this indefinable phrase. However, after the publication of the Warren 'Report,' many commentators and historians interpret that phrase to mean that whenever a future president is murdered his killers can escape capture and punishment if a future investigating committee decides their capture would be 'against the national interest.'"

Second, Marks accurately predicts how the lies of the Warren Commission (WC) will affect the collective national psyche in the decades to come. At the end of *Murder Most Foul!*, in a chapter titled "The Rape of the American Conscience," he writes: "It can now be said that the American people do not believe anything stated in the 'Report.' Due to this lack of belief, a cynicism has now gathered among the citizenry that bodes ill for the nation. A nation whose moral fiber has been torn and shattered cannot long live; for when the nation's spirit is destroyed, no nation will live." Reflecting on this passage, DiEugenio adds that Marks sounded "a note that no other critic of that time voiced."[52]

What exactly gave birth to this cynicism? In the author's own words, "The American Creed, which is expressed in the Preamble to the Constitution of the United States, has been violated, and this violation has been condoned by the Warren

---

[52] In *Coup d'État* Marks plays with a variation on this theme by stating: "Not only did they deliberately conceal the conspiracy but they committed a rape of the American conscience. There can be no forgiving when that rape destroyed the soul of the nation."

Commission." Marks emphasizes the fact that the principle elements enumerated in the Preamble – *justice, domestic tranquility, promoting the general welfare*, and *securing liberty* – were blasphemously profaned by the conspirators and the Commissioners (at least one of which – Allen Dulles – may have served in each of these roles). Therefore, the Commission's message to the American people is that justice, domestic tranquility, promoting the general welfare, and securing liberty can no longer be taken for granted. "People, in all nations," Marks continues, "must stand for an ideal. The United States of America was not born on the idea that its President could be shot like a dog in the street and his murderers be 'shielded from this day on' because it would be 'against the national interests.' The Spirit has in this year of 1967 been replaced by cynicism of everything 'American.' […] How long, oh how long, Americans, will we permit our silence to perpetuate the evil in the Warren Report?"

Citing such passages, DiEugenio concludes: "This condemnation is a far cry from Josiah Thompson, who, at the end of his book, said he was not really sure that the evidence he adduced justified a conspiracy." Commenting on this passage again during an interview conducted by Len Osanic in April 2020, DiEugenio adds: "It even goes beyond, polemically, what Sylvia Meagher wrote. I'd have to put that up there with Mark Lane, who ended his book by saying something like, This report is so bad that is shames the people who defend it as much as it does the people who criticize it." And to accomplish this, Marks utilizes an incisive no-holds-barred polemical style that is completely unique for its period.

Third, during a time when it was considered highly unfashionable to do so, "Marks again does something that neither Meagher nor Thompson did – quite the contrary. He praises and appreciates the efforts of New Orleans District

Attorney Jim Garrison. He compares Garrison's ordeal against the media to St. George galloping forth to duel with the dragon." (The postscript of *Murder Most Foul!* is even titled: "Jim Garrison, 'St. George' Versus the 'Dragon'!")

Fourth, Marks "says something quite prescient for the time: he accuses some of Garrison's attackers of being in bed with the CIA. Which, we now know, is an accurate assessment."

Marks immediately recognized the valiant efforts of Jim Garrison, who was being attacked not only by WC supporters but also by many WC critics on the left, including many of the most prominent assassination researchers. And the true nature of this state-sponsored dragon and what it was capable of accomplishing – by whatever means necessary – was also apparent to Stanley Marks. He opens his Postscript by stating:

By the time this book appears in print, the Kennedy conspiracy may claim another victim: none other than Jim Garrison, the district attorney of New Orleans, whose "lance of truth" has pierced vital organs of the conspiracy that murdered President F. Kennedy.

There is no question that Mr. Garrison's investigation has created a firm base in the theory that President Kennedy was the victim of the Batista backed anti-Castro groups in the United States. These groups, in turn, have the full support of the CIA.

The mass communication media, many of its organs either being paid by the CIA or having its agents in executive positions, have entered the battle against Mr. Garrison's efforts to reveal the existence of the conspiracy.

Never in the history of American journalism has the entire mass communication media entered into a plan to destroy, not only a case, but the person conducting the prosecution of a criminal case. In addition, this is being done on a national scale. [...]

Various members of the mass communication media bribed witnesses, hid witnesses, issued fraudulent interviews, had "witnesses" file suit against Mr. Garrison, produced nationwide television programs which upheld the findings of the Warren Commission. How incredible! Why?

The answer to "why" can be found in the fact that many of the inactive and active participants of the conspiracy will be found in the ranks of the government and the economic strata of our nation.

Here Marks introduces what might be regarded as a "quintessence" placed at a central point between the four cornerstones. That is, the role of the ruling economic elite that exists one level above the intelligence agencies and that utilizes the media to broadcast its narrative, sell its products, and guarantee its remunerative investments in the war machine. This concept was rarely broached by assassination researchers other than Jim Garrison until Fletcher Prouty (the Pentagon's former liaison officer to the CIA) published *The Secret Team* in 1972. This same line of thought was later probed by author Donald Gibson, whose insights on the subject were assembled into articles such as "The Creation of the Warren Commission" (1997) and later expanded in *Battling Wall Street* (1994) and *The Kennedy Assassination Cover-up* (2000). But Marks raises this issue throughout his oeuvre, and he neatly sums it up with just a couple of sentences in the Postscript when he asks: "To whom does the mass communication system owe its loyalty? To the people who have fought, are fighting, and will continue to fight for the ideas of the 'freedom of the press,' or to its advertisers?"

Thus, in going that extra step of recognizing the deeper

currents that remained invisible to so many other authors in 1967, he again lays much of the blame on the media, pointing to their culpability, their infiltration by the CIA, and their subservience to the economic forces that rule the nation. "That the CIA controls many of the news columns in both the press and magazines is now known. What is not known, and what will never be known, is how many agents of the CIA now work for various organs in the mass communication media." How many people thinking about this in 1967?

As a point of comparison, we might add that in *Six Seconds in Dallas* Josiah Thompson never once discusses the CIA. In Thompson's account, the phrase "Central Intelligence Agency" appears only in a letter written by FBI Director Hoover, which is reproduced in the book's appendix along with other National Archives documents but minus any commentary by Thompson. In marked contrast, Marks doesn't waste any time in introducing the subject of the Agency and in trying to grapple with where and to what extent we may find its tentacles entangled in the case. In chapter two of *Murder Most Foul!* he asks: "Was Oswald any type of an agent for the CIA? The evidence is accumulating that the answer is 'yes.'"

He also doesn't hesitate to examine the role of former CIA Director Dulles in both the plot and the cover-up. First, he excoriates Dulles for a widely quoted remark that Dulles made to a journalist in 1966: "If they found another assassin, let them name names and produce their evidence." Marks reacts forcefully and unflinchingly when he replies to Dulles: "This contemptuous statement directed at the American citizenry revealed the attitude of the Commission. The Commission did not praise the president; they gave him a funeral and used his shroud to conceal his murderers." Then he asks: "Mr. Dulles, how can other assassins be named if material is *not* in the National Archives? Was there a conspiracy, Mr. Dulles? Of course there was!"

Marks also explores the agency's role in the plot: "The inception of the conspiracy that murdered President Kennedy can be, and will be eventually, traced back to the disastrous 'Bay of Pigs.' The president relied upon the CIA, headed by Allen Dulles, whose information was one hundred percent wrong in the CIA's assessment of Castro's Cuba. Heads rolled but the CIA had many heads and the heads that remained never forgave President Kennedy [...] Thus, in the wreckage of the 'Bay of Pigs' were parts and persons of the CIA apparatus who had directed that operation. The hatred of this apparatus for President Kennedy was to cease only when these forces fired four bullets into his body."

He then returns to the subject of JFK's foreign policy, which he views as the most likely reason for the assassination:

> With the relaxation of tensions between the U.S. and the USSR after President Kennedy's confrontation with the Soviets in the Cuban Missile Crisis, the Batista–Cuban exile organization, with many members on the CIA payroll, decided that Kennedy must go. However, the murder of President Kennedy was the "spark," a means to an end.
>
> The Kennedy conspiracy had a major and minor objective: (1) An invasion of Cuba; (2) an attempt to involve the Soviet Union with the invasion so that a war would ensue between the U.S. and USSR.
>
> By early 1963, members of the Conspiracy, who were both U.S. citizens and exiled Cubans of the Batista faction, had been selected.

After presenting his case, composed of over nine hundred questions and answers in the style of an attorney cross-examining a witness, at the very end of *Murder Most Foul!* he again returns to Dulles' contemptuous remark. "No, Mr. Dulles," Marks concludes, "it was not the responsibility of the American citizen to find and name the assassins; that was your task. Your lack of responsibility to the task is the cause for your failure. You issued the 'Report' under your name; you had at your disposal the entire operating machinery of the government of the United States. We citizens have only what you and your fellow Commissioners wrote. We read, we looked, we analyzed, we thought; and we, nearly seventy percent of us, now deliver a verdict on your work: The Warren Commission was a failure." Thus Marks turns the tables on the CIA director and on the Commission itself, suggesting that the ones who should be the subject of an investigation and report are the Commissioners themselves, who served as puppets for the military industrial complex.

In the Postscript's conclusion the author places a capstone upon a prediction that will come to pass: "If the forces behind the conspiracy cannot destroy Mr. Garrison's case they may decide to destroy the man, either physically or by reputation." Not only did the Establishment sully Garrison's reputation and commit a character assassination with the help of the CIA. They also convinced many of the leading researchers that Garrison was a source of embarrassment and that, by supporting him, they could only sully their own reputation. It wasn't until Oliver Stone's dramatic portrayal of Garrison in his film *JFK* that the public was offered a qualitatively different image of this heroic figure, whose pioneering work was light years beyond that of those same researchers who disgracefully turned their backs on his groundbreaking efforts to uncover the truth.

In January 1968 the *Berkeley Barb* (an underground paper known for its combination of psychedelia and radical politics) featured a half-page review of *Murder Most Foul!* that can still be accessed online. In the spirit of the time the reviewer uses the phrase "mind-blowing"; favorably compares *Murder Most Foul!* to William Manchester's *Death of a President* (referring to the latter as an "epic rationalization that Oswald killed Kennedy"); and ends with a suggestion: "Read Marks' book and toss and turn the rest of the night."[53]

The following month Elliot Mintz, an "underground DJ" at KPFK radio in LA, produced "a special in-depth probe … concerning the assassination of John F. Kennedy and the investigation by New Orleans District Attorney Jim Garrison." A program brochure lists an interview with Stanley as well as interviews with prominent researchers such as Harold Weisberg, Penn Jones, Maggie Field, and Ray Marcus; and a "Round table discussion with assassination experts." Comedian-activist Mort Sahl was also included in the show.[54] (When I contacted Mintz in 2020, he said that he had no recollection of interviewing Stanley; so it's likely the interview was conducted by another journalist and subsequently featured in the broadcast.)

For the next thirty-two years Marks managed to publish an additional twenty-two books: an average of about one every year and a half. Five months after the appearance of *Murder Most Foul!*, in February 1968 he copyrighted his first play about the assassination: an eighty-one page manuscript titled "A Murder Most Foul! Or, A Time to Die, A Time to Cry," which he describes as "a three-act play that reveals how a chief of state

---

[53] *Berkeley Barb*, January 12, 1968, p. 10 (unsigned and untitled).

[54] This information comes from a KPFK Radio programming pamphlet published in March 1968. Marks is also mentioned as a program guest in Mintz's article, "Looking Out," *Los Angeles Free Press*, March 1, 1968, p. 24.

was assassinated." This is the first of several dramatic works penned by the author, all of them political in nature. As various copyright registrations attest to, he continued to fiddle with this particular play, revising and expanding it. By 1970 it was described as "A three-act play concerning the three murders that changed the course of history: President Kennedy, Martin Luther King, and Senator Robert F. Kennedy."[55]

In January 1969 Meredith Press published Paris Flammonde's *The Kennedy Conspiracy: An Uncommissioned Report on the Jim Garrison Investigation*: the first reliable, in-depth examination of Jim Garrison's ongoing case against Clay Shaw for his role in the conspiracy. Although it received reviews in the mainstream media, predictably most of them were negative, since the author was critical of the Warren Commission and supportive of Garrison's efforts. *The Kennedy Conspiracy* also features a select, two-page bibliography that lists Stanley's *Murder Most Foul!* alongside the work of more well-known WC critics such as Penn Jones, Mark Lane, Sylvia Meagher, and Harold Weisberg.

Despite the negative press, Flammonde's study proved to be a classic in the field. It also chronicles Garrison's thoughts on matters such as Clay Shaw's role in the CIA-front organizations known as Centro Mondiale Commerciale and Permindex. Jim DiEugenio, who spearheaded the movement to sweep past the poisonous accusations hurled at Garrison and to set his remarkable record straight, later said: "My first book would not

---

[55] In the spring of 2021 I was able to retrieve copies of the original 1968 play about JFK and the expanded 1979 version (the latter titled: "A Time to Die, A Time to Cry, or, Murders Most Foul!"). A final version of "A Time to Die, A Time to Cry" was deposited in the Copyright Office in 1988 but has since been reported as "lost."

exist in the form it does without Paris Flammonde."[56] Since Garrison was in frequent contact with Flammonde and presumably received a copy of his book, it's tempting to speculate on whether Garrison – a voracious reader – ever purchased a copy of *Murder Most Foul!* after spotting it in Flammonde's bibliography.

In March 1969 Marks published his second JFK study, *Two Days of Infamy: November 22, 1963; September 28, 1964*. Though it was published just two months after *The Kennedy Conspiracy*, he cites Flammonde's work throughout this text. The subtitle refers to the dates of the JFK assassination and the release of the WC Report. Here Marks once again explores the miscarriage of justice in the "dark world" of the JFK case. He adds that although this shadowy realm is "slowly, oh, so slowly, being lit," he wonders if "full light may take until the year 2038 – if the 'basic principles of American justice' have the strength to remain as principles guiding this long-suffering nation."[57] Marks also returns to the theme of cynicism and despair that was first raised in such a prophetic manner in *Murder Most Foul!* In *Two Days of Infamy* he writes:

> Perhaps it was the cynicism, inherent in citizens of all nations, that convinced the American citizenry that the "Report" issued by the Warren Commission was supported by rotten timbers incapable of supporting the truth. The suspicion increased in the same ratio and in the same speed as smog increased with the density of

---

[56] James DiEugenio, "Honor to Paris Flammonde," Kennedys and King website, January 24, 2015.
[57] The unpublished Warren Commission records were initially sealed for 75 years (until 2039).

automobiles on a Los Angeles freeway. The American people were becoming deeply convinced that the Commission had perpetrated a gigantic, gruesome hoax the like of which concealed a conspiracy that reached into the very gut of American government and society. Today, that hoax, that whitewash feared by the people has been exposed to the light of day, for the citizenry were, and are, absolutely right in their assessment of the Warren Commission. There now exists overwhelming evidence, provable in a court of law, that the Warren Commission, either willfully or negligently, concealed the conspiracy that murdered President John F. Kennedy. This deed was committed by the Commission in "the interests of national security."

Directly connected to this cynicism is another deadly poison: the corruption of the corporate media, leading to the public's loss of faith in any "official story." In *Murder Most Foul!* he addresses the infiltration of the mass communication systems by the CIA; in *Two Days of Infamy* he adds: "The investigators of the 'Report' have presented the result of their investigations to the public; but the silence of the press lords to further an investigation of the Commission's allegations has led to a further decline of the general public's faith in all forms of mass communication." Thus, the media's betrayal of its own subscribers ultimately backfires and destroys any sense of collective well-being. But Marks goes on to blame not only the usual suspects in the Deep Establishment but also the WC critics themselves:

The critics' primary failure was their repeated implication that the murder of President Kennedy could not

be solved unless, at the same time, they proved a conspiracy. The critics have constantly proclaimed that
unless the Zapruder film, the X-Rays, and other photo-
graphic evidence was released from the National
Archives, no solution could be obtained. Their de-
mands obscure the main issue: "Was Lee Harvey
Oswald the 'sole and exclusive assassin of President
Kennedy' as charged by the Warren Commission?"

The contents of this passage are reminiscent of the work of
another prescient researcher who plumbed the depths of the
case: Vincent Salandria, who once warned investigator Gaeton
Fonzi: "I'm afraid we were misled. All the critics, myself
included, were misled very early. I see that now. We spent too
much time and effort microanalyzing the details of the assassination when all the time it was obvious, it was blatantly obvious that it was a conspiracy." Salandria felt that such a
"microanalysis" would only serve to trap the researchers in the
crucible of Dealey Plaza. But those with a wider range of vision
and a deeper sense of history might see past this illusion; for,
only a "macro" historical perspective would allow us to use the
past to accurately predict future trends. And this is how Marks
grapples with what may lie in store:

> History has proven that once assassination has become
> the weapon to change the government, that style and
> form of government preceding the assassination falls
> beneath the hard-nailed boots of the assassins. Both
> right and left favor no democratic spirit in the people.
> The cold of Siberia and the gas ovens of the concentra-
> tion camps have proved it.
> The tragedy of the Warren Commission is that they
> helped set those boots on the road to the destruction of

American democracy.

He concludes that all this could only occur because the citizens of the U.S. are "living in a dream world concocted by the mass communication systems."[58]

Two Days of Infamy eventually came to the attention of Mary Ferrell, a figure that many in the research community have come to regard with a great deal of suspicion. In a group letter from January 13, 1970 addressed to several of her colleagues, she writes: "Mr. Marks is a little off the track on a number of things, but there is enough in it that is interesting to make it worthwhile having." Since Ferrell was averse to anyone proposing the idea that the CIA and the national security state had anything to do with the assassination (she instead pushed the hypothesis that Texas oil interests and Lyndon Johnson were behind it, thus drawing attention away from the Agency), this could explain her caveat to Stanley's work. But another notable assassination researcher, Penn Jones, quoted from *Two Days of Infamy* without any such reservations. (More on Jones below.)

Eleven months later, in February 1970, *Two Days of Infamy* was followed by Marks' third nonfiction work on the case, *Coup d'État! Three Murders That Changed the Course of History. President Kennedy, Reverend King, Senator R. F. Kennedy*. That same month the *Los Angeles Free Press* published an article titled "Assassination Story Slowly Disintegrates"[59] that prominently features material from *Coup d'État!* It also highlights Marks'

[58] Some of these passages are reproduced word for word in Mark's next JFK title, *Coup d'État*.
[59] "Assassination Story Slowly Disintegrates," *Los Angeles Free Press*, February 18, 1920, p. 20.

discussion about how Dallas Police Chief Jesse Curry was now admitting that he'd given a press conference shortly after the assassination in which he'd stated that none of Oswald's fingerprints or palm prints were found on the rifle, and that there weren't any witnesses who could place Oswald "at the same sixth-floor window prior, during, or after the president's murder."

*　　*　　*

Shortly after Chile's Salvador Allende became the first Marxist president in Latin America (assuming office on November 30, 1970), Stanley published his critical attack on the Nixon presidency, *Watch What We Do ... Not What We Say!* (1971). He describes it as an "account of the present trend of the Nixon – Agnew – Mitchell – Southern strategy axis" and "the possibility of Orwell's '1984' being accomplished by 1972." During a discussion on the dangers of the CIA ("It can, and does, murder both foreign and national leaders"), almost as an aside he accurately predicts what will happen next in Chile. And he does so by comparing the fate of Chile to that of Vietnam:

> After the extermination of the Indo-Chinese nations as nations, the CIA will then proceed to "exterminate" another nation – Chile. The Establishment's propaganda is already being published with the same old trite and dreary slogans: "The Chileans pose a threat to our security." A nation that is more than 5,000 miles away from the territorial mainland of the United States, with no navy, army, or air force that cannot even drop leaflets on our mainland!
>
> Thus, with the CIA "protecting" the people from "invasions" and the FBI maintaining its ever-vigilant

status over the "dissenters," the people calmly lockstep
their way into a prison of their own making.[60]

Two years after this was published, on September 11, 1973 the
CIA organized and staged the coup that would overthrow the
democratically elected government of Allende and usher in a
murderous right-wing dictator, General Pinochet, who dis-
solved all remnants of democracy and replaced them with a
military junta that ruled by fear, torture, and the "disappear-
ance" of those who had the courage to resist. Stanley saw it
coming because his research had trained him to recognize
broader historical patterns.[61] Although none dare call it "extermination," he was right about that as well: The CIA did conduct
extermination. In this same text Marks would further elaborate
on the connection between politics and economics that he first
explored in *Murder Most Foul!* In a chapter titled "The
Establishment" he writes: "It can be said that not more than
8,000 persons [...] comprise the Establishment. They control
every major decision, foreign and domestic, made in the nation.
It is not a 'conspiracy' but a 'meeting of the minds.' They
sincerely believe that 'what is good for them is good for the
country.'"

This book also came to the attention of author Penn Jones. In
volume three of Jones' *Forgive My Grief* series, he writes: "We
urge you to read the new bestseller, *Future Shock* by Alan Toffler;
and *Watch What We Do ... Not What We Say* by Stanley J.
Marks ... Both will frighten you, but they are important books.

---

[60] Stanley and Ethel Marks, *Watch What We Do ... Not What We Say!*,
Los Angeles: Bureau of International Affairs, 1971, p. 157.
[61] Reminiscent of a line from Henri Barbusse's classic World War I
novel, *Under Fire*: "Ah, he has looked too deeply into the profundity
of the past not to see the future with appalling accuracy."

That is, if you care which way we are going."

In 1972 Marks published his first work on the history of religion and politics, *Through Distorted Mirrors!* Both the German-American philosopher Herbert Marcuse and the British historian Arnold Toynbee endorsed the text, and their blurbs are reproduced on its back cover. That same year Stanley was mentioned in Joachim Joesten's mimeographed "Truth Letter" broadsheet: "To my knowledge nobody but Jim Garrison (and an obscure West Coast writer named Stanley J. Marks) has ever endorsed before my unswerving contention that the murder of John F. Kennedy was nothing short of a camouflaged coup d'état."[62] (A prolific author, Joesten's book *Oswald: Assassin or Fall Guy?* was one of the primary sources of information that Stanley relied upon while writing *Murder Most Foul!*) Thus, he was gradually coming to the attention of several prominent figures.

But perhaps the most unexpected acknowledgment of his work came on March 12, 1973, when the JFK Library contacted Marks (through the office of the U.S. General Services Administration) with a request to purchase a copy of *Murder Most Foul!* for their collection. At that time Robert Kennedy's trusted colleague, Dave Powers (who had served as JFK's personal assistant) had been placed in charge of assembling materials for the library. Powers believed that JFK had been shot by an assassin stationed in front of the presidential limousine, which might explain the library's interest in purchasing the work of a conspiracy researcher. Still, it's hard to imagine how they first learned of this little-known self-published book.

---

[62] Joachim Joesten, "Truth Letter," Gutenberg, Germany (self-published mimeograph), May 1, 1972, p. 4.

By the late 1970s several other footnotes of recognition appear in Stanley's biography. Tom Miller's *The Assassination Please Almanac* (1977) contains brief mentions of *Murder Most Foul!* (noting that it was "hard to find"), *Two Days of Infamy, Coup d'État!, Watch What We Do ... Not What We Say!,* and a 1971 version of Marks' play, "A Time to Die, A Time to Cry." And in March 1979 five of his books were indexed by the House Select Committee on Assassinations in its report, "The Assassination of President John F. Kennedy: A Chronological Bibliography."[63] The same five titles (including *Murder Most Foul!*) were listed in the "Library of Congress Comprehensive JFK Assassination Bibliography," which was completed that same month.

Over the next two decades Marks published several works that were highly critical of the Reagan administration and that probed the Iran–Contra affair. These include titles such as *A Year in the Lives of the Damned! Reagan, Reaganism, 1986* ("written in the form of a diary; each month is a chapter"; 1988); *The Defeat, Dishonor, and Disgrace! The Reagan–Bush Regimes* (1993); and *If This be Treason...!* ("The truth of how citizens Reagan, Bush, Casey, and their friends betrayed and destroyed the Carter administration in the 1980 presidential election"; 1996).

Having lived in California during Reagan's reign there as governor, Marks was a long-term critic of the future president, even calling him to task in 1967 in *Murder Most Foul!* In the February 1968 version of his three-act play about the JFK assassination, one of the characters utters a prophetic warning: "Don't underestimate him [Governor Ronald Reagan]. He may one day become our Chief of State." In *A Year in the Lives of the Damned!*, while discussing Reagan's contempt for the poor and disenfranchised, Stanley quotes from JFK's inaugural: "If a free society cannot help the many who are poor, it cannot save the

---

[63]See volume 12, p. 695.

few who are rich." He then identifies the author of the quote: "A Twentieth-Century Radical: John F. Kennedy. The President of the U.S.!" During this period he also published the *Diogenes* newsletter (a political screed), several pages of which are reproduced in his books about the Reagan–Bush era.

Marks would not return to the subject of the assassination until the early 1990s. After viewing Oliver Stone's film *JFK*, in June 1992 he published his last major work on the case: *Yes, Americans, A Conspiracy Murdered JFK!* As with his earlier studies, the text is notable for going far beyond a mere microanalysis of the Dealey Plaza drama. On the one hand, he never fails to include a careful examination of the forensic evidence, or to discuss the conflicting statements that appear on various government documents, or to utilize an attorney's unique frame of reference and hone in on key points that don't add up under the scrutiny of common sense. (E.g., as he reiterates in *Yes, Americans*: "As a defense attorney, my best witness would be the Warren Commission's "Report" and the 26 volumes issued by the Commission.") But on the other hand, all this eventually leads to a larger, "bigger picture" perspective that is cogently shaped by the author's view that the president's foreign policy initiatives were the principal reason for his demise. In this final work on the assassination, Marks ties the strands of economics and media into a single statement: "Many persons cannot understand the reason why the powerful newspapers and the ABC, CBS, and NBC television and radio chains have kept a constant drumbeat against the critics of the Warren Commission. The reason is quite simple – when the president was murdered the power structure shifted both economically and politically." He concludes that this was accomplished with the assistance of the FBI and CIA, both of which he refers to as "a state within a state." Stanley is unwittingly echoing the words of Arthur Schlesinger, Jr. who, on June 30, 1961, authored a twelve-page memo to President Kennedy (which still remains partially redacted). Under the title "CIA Reorganization," Schlesinger warns the president that the Agency is operating far too independently. On the very first page of this report Schlesinger notes "The argument of this memorandum is that CIA's trouble can be traced to the autonomy with which the agency has been permitted to operate ..." On page three he concludes: "The contemporary CIA possesses many of the characteristics of a state within a state," adding: "The result of CIA's initiative in covert political operations has been known to create situations which have forced policy on the State Department. This was not the original idea behind CIA. [...] CIA has, in effect, 'made' policy in many parts of the world."[64]

One wonders what would have stopped the Agency from "forcing policy" upon us domestically via a carefully crafted presidential assassination and cover-up: the very specialty that the Agency became known for the world over.

Three years before his death at the age of eighty-five, Marks published a thirty-six page paperback, *Justice for Whom?* (1996), which chronicles "five Americans whose criminal or civil trials engaged the attention of millions of people." One of the five is Lee Oswald. The passage on Oswald is only four pages long and titled: "The Oswald Trial by Commission, or the 'Assassin' Who Assassinated No One." Here, Marks returns to the role of an attorney who remains focused on the reasons why, in a fair trial, Lee could not have been convicted of being the "sole assassin and exclusive assassin" in the murder of the president:

---

[64] See National Archives and Records Administration (NARA) record number 176-10030-10422, Sorensen Papers, archives.com.

The press and the columnists for TV, radio, and print for years have successfully implanted in the minds of many Americans that those who claimed that a conspiracy murdered the president were "paranoiac" and to "trust their government," i.e., the Warren Commission.

Thus, the supporters of the Commission impliedly called "liars" the FBI personnel who wrote many FBI statements that proved the Oswald rifle was so imperfect that the FBI's own marksmen refused to fire that Oswald rifle until the FBI ballistic department repaired the defective rifle! The "nonparanoiac" columnists refused to believe the various written statements by J. Edgar Hoover informing the Commission that the rifle bullets or cartridges given to the FBI by the Dallas Police or Sheriff's Department did not fit within that Oswald rifle. Nor did the "sane" columnists defending the Warren Commission know that the Oswald palm print published in the Warren Report was a flat palm print, not a curved print of a person grasping a rifle barrel or its stock that was alleged to be used by the rifleman.

The appearance of this essay near the end of the author's life attests to both his enduring fascination with the case as well as his lingering and righteous indignation over the injustices that came to pass on November 22, 1963.

Marks circa 1934. When he was four years old, he lost his parents to the 1918 influenza pandemic. Roberta Marks recalls her father saying that "he never had enough food. When you see pictures of him as a youth, he was bone-thin and skinny. That is, until he married my mother, whose cooking he adored." Stanley's experience with hunger on Chicago's hardscrabble streets may have helped to open his eyes to a certain political awareness and to mold him into a lifelong FDR New Dealer.

Ethel Milgrom and Stanley Marks, circa 1936.

Above: Yearbook photo of the "Debater's Forum" at John Marshall Law School. Marks is standing third from the left.

Next page: Private Marks at an army base library, circa 1945. By his late twenties Marks had accumulated a private collection of over 5,000 books.

Stanley with his daughter Roberta at Union Pier, Michigan, circa 1950. He later inscribed a copy of his book *Two Days of Infamy* "To my daughter Bobbie, *the* apple in my orchard and the filament in the bulb of her parent's life. With Love Daddy"

UNITED STATES OF AMERICA
GENERAL SERVICES ADMINISTRATION

National Archives and Records Service
John F. Kennedy Library
380 Trapelo Road
Waltham, Massachusetts 02154

Telephone: 617 223-7250

March 12, 1973

Bureau of International Affairs
6769 W. Lexington Avenue
Los Angeles, CA 90038

Gentlemen:

The Kennedy Library is interested in acquiring the
book listed below from your company. Please consider
this letter our order and bill us accordingly.

Marks, Stanley J.

MURDER MOST FOUL. 1967

Our purchase order number is: JB-NLK-147. If
you would be kind enough to send the book and
invoice to my attention, it would be much appreciated.

Thank you in advance for your cooperation in this
matter.

Sincerely,

JOAN BARONIAN
Purchasing Agent

Keep Freedom in Your Future With U.S. Savings Bonds

**In 1973 the John F. Kennedy Library contacted Marks with a request to
purchase a copy of *Murder Most Foul!* for their collection.**

Afterword by James DiEugenio

Many people underestimate the importance and value of serendipity in life. But it is due to serendipity that you have just read this play in book form. The reason you did is because of a rather famous songwriter named Bob Dylan.

In March of 2020, Dylan released his song about the murder of President Kennedy. The impact of that rather long ballad was immediate and powerful. How many songs actually have magazine and newspaper columns written about them? How many are downloaded two million times in four days? The title of that elegiac, almost seventeen-minute lyric was *Murder Most Foul*. Although the song was about the murder of President Kennedy, it took its title from Shakespeare's *Hamlet*.

But as far as I know, Rob Couteau was the first, and perhaps only, commentator to note that: Maybe Dylan did not borrow the phrase directly from Shakespeare. Maybe he read the 1967 volume by Stanley Marks which had the same title, *Murder Most Foul!* Although the work of Stanley Marks is noted in the House Select Committee on Assassinations' volumes, and this particular book was ordered by the JFK Library, not many people recalled Stanley Marks or his work. Why?

Unlike the early critics – of which he was one – Stanley did not have a major, or even a medium-sized publisher releasing his work. This difference should be noted as we make some comparisons with other first-generation critics of the Warren Commission Report. Sylvia Meagher had The Bobbs-Merrill Company; Mark Lane had Holt, Rinehart and Winston; Josiah Thompson had Bernard Geis Associates and Random House; Edward Epstein had The Viking Press. Except for the first, these were all New York based publishing houses who could put some torque behind the release of their product. (Bobbs-Merrill was based in Indianapolis.) Therefore, mentioning just two examples, Thompson's *Six Seconds in Dallas* was excerpted in *The Saturday Evening Post*, and Lane's *Rush to Judgment* spent twenty-nine weeks as a top-ten bestseller.

As Rob Couteau describes elsewhere, Stanley Marks' *Murder Most Foul!* was self-published. Which means he had to pay for the print costs and any promotion of the book himself. What is extraordinary about this is that, as Couteau also points out, Stanley's book actually did get some notices in the smaller press. In my opinion, it should not only have gotten more notices from larger-circulation media, but, in addition, the writers should have noted the difference between Stanley's work and what Epstein, Thompson, Lane, and Meagher were doing. (We could also add Harold Weisberg here, since his book *Whitewash* got a paperback release by the Dell Publishing Company of New York.)

What would have been notable if such a comparison had been done? First, Stanley's approach was different. He was a graduate of the John Marshall Law School in Chicago, which today is part of the University of Illinois. So for his analysis, he used the British / European inquisitorial magistrate method, which is one of questioning by the judge of the prosecutor's case. In this phase, it is the judge who decides if the accused is the perpetrator and if the case should go to trial. If he decides that no crime was committed, or the accused was not the perpetrator, the case does not go to trial.

Attorney Stanley Marks was one of the very few people in America who read both the 888 page Warren Commission Report and the accompanying twenty-six volumes of testimony and exhibits. Out of that mountain of material, his book features 975 questions for the prosecution. In a relentless and blistering manner, he showed why the case against Oswald should not go to trial. In other words, he stopped the Commission right out of the starting gate. And that is also a difference between Stanley and the other early critics.

For instance, the subtitle of Meagher's *Accessories After the Fact* is "The Warren Commission, the Authorities, and the Report." Weisberg's is "The Report on the Warren Report." Epstein's *Inquest* is "The Warren Commission and the Establishment of Truth." All three are fairly mild. Especially in comparison with attorney Stanley Marks', which is: "The Conspiracy That Murdered President Kennedy." In other words, for Stanley, he did not want to go through any kind of expository style of presenting one side against the other and then pointing to what was left out.

A good example of this is the opening chapter of *Murder Most Foul!* That chapter is entitled "To Dallas We Go." Right out of the starting blocks, Marks dives into an area that was rarely dealt with by most writers, if at all. Namely, the absurd motorcade route: who had knowledge of it and – something that is really startling that Stanley brings up – whether or not the limousine stopped in Dealey Plaza while negotiating the extremely sharp turns (p. 166). That particular question did not really surface with any real force until about twenty years later, particularly with Jim Garrison and his *On the Trail of the Assassins*. Yet Marks begins his 1967 book with it. Marks, as magisterial judge, wants to know: Who approved this route? Was it the Secret Service? Or was it the local police? Or are they trying to slough it off on each other?

Marks clearly perceives this as quite crucial to the Kennedy case. As he does another matter: The other people who were arrested that day (p. 169). In the next chapter Marks again goes longer than any of the first-generation critics, this time on the subject of Lee Harvey Oswald. He declares flatly that Oswald was an informant for the FBI and an agent of the CIA (p. 174).

I could go on and on about the critical acuity and comprehensiveness of Stanley Marks' work and how it differs in kind from that of other first-generation critics. I would encourage the reader to do that on his own. But I will point out two more general subjects which Stanley Marks deals with that the others did not, at least in public.

First, Stanley made no bones about the irresponsibility of the mass media in regards to the assassination. Again, this is made clear very early in that first book, specifically in chapter two. In question #72, Marks asks, "What value were the NBC and CBS programs in 1967?" If the reader will recall, those two programs were: (1) A one hour prime-time program on New Orleans DA Jim Garrison hosted by Frank McGee, and (2) A four hour, four-night endorsement of the Warren Report co-hosted by Walter Cronkite and Dan Rather.

The first program was broadcast by NBC on June 19, 1967. The second one began a week later and aired from June 25–28. The NBC program was an out-and-out hatchet job on New Orleans DA Jim Garrison. It was so bad that when Garrison petitioned for time to reply under the Fairness Doctrine, it was granted. Years later, using material stolen from CBS by employee Roger Feinman, this writer was allowed to show just how dishonest the CBS program actually was. To the point that it violated its own Standards and Practices doctrines. (See the article "How CBS News Aided the JFK Cover-up" at *Consortium News*.)

Stanley answered his question about what value those two shows had like this:

> No value except that the programs revealed the
> awesome power of the FBI and CIA to compel the
> mass communication media to intercede on behalf
> of the Warren Commission … and both systems

proved that its interpretation of "freedom of the press" in 1967 is not Jefferson's of 1776. The CBS "rifle" tests and "bullet" tests were as phony as phony could be.

There was no being careful about this matter by Mr. Marks. And the documentation that was later revealed about both shows prove him out. (For specifics about the NBC program, see William Davy's book, *Let Justice be Done*, pp. 135-38.)

The other point about which Stanley was way ahead of everyone else was this: His sense that this was – clearly and fundamentally – a political crime. He says the originating cause of the crime was the failed Bay of Pigs invasion of 1961. He then outlines what he thinks actually happened to enact that conspiracy. And again, if the experienced reader can comprehend it, Red Bird Airfield is part of his outline (pp. 359-65). You will not find anything like this in the other examples I have cited.

And neither will you find anything like his chapter thirteen. Entitled "The Rape of the American Conscience," here he states that what the Warren Commission did was to rip the moral fiber from underneath the country: "A Nation whose moral fiber has been torn and shattered cannot long live: for when the Nation's spirit is destroyed no Nation will live" (p. 353).

He goes on to say that cynicism has taken over the national psyche, in large part because the mass of the public does not believe the Warren Report. He then writes:

There was a Spirit when John F. Kennedy was president of the United States. There was a feeling that the United States of America was moving toward a goal enunciated in the Preamble of the Constitution.

But now, he went on, that American Creed of the Constitution "has been violated and this violation has been condoned by the Warren Commission." He concludes that chapter with this: "How long, oh how long, Americans, will we permit our silence to perpetuate the evil in the Warren Report?"

Because that evil never left our nation, for Stanley, this was a cause that he could never forsake. And he was writing books and pamphlets on the subject into the Nineties. That is when Oliver Stone's film *JFK* brought the subject back to life for a younger generation.

What is so remarkable about Stanley is that his analytical efforts were not enough for the man. He attempted to bring this heinous crime to the attention of the public through his efforts as a playwright. And, thanks to Couteau, we now have his play about the assassination of President Kennedy.

In the Preface to this play, called *A Murder Most Foul: Or A Time to Cry, A Time to Die,* Stanley repeats his ideas about the assassination. He writes that the Bay of Pigs was the ignition switch which sent Kennedy to death in a hail of bullets. He then says that those bullets not only killed Kennedy "but also the soul and vision that represented the ideal of the United States of America."

The play is an interesting effort. For instance, the first two scenes have no dialogue, not even a monologue. The first scene is actually done with no actors onstage. It is designed to set a mood in total darkness, one of violence and tragedy. So we get wailing voices, the sounds of rifle fire, and police sirens. It then concludes with music from a funeral procession, three shots being fired, and the trumpeting of Taps.

The next scene is meant to be partly symbolic. The controller of the plot to kill JFK – simply named King – comes into a room which is adorned with the flags of Texas and the Confederacy. The fireplace has a mantle with a decorative oil derrick on top.

He takes out a golf bag and places two rifles inside. He then opens up a compartment in the bag to stuff in bullets. King then wipes the golf bag clean and walks it to the door. An unseen person takes the bag from him. He turns around, walks to the bar and pours himself a drink. He consumes the drink, closes the lights, and walks out.

Again, nothing has been said so far. And the two scenes are chronologically reversed. It is the second scene that actually caused the first one. Momentous events – namely the preparations for and the execution of an assassination – have all been done in silence. And the plot was successful.

The action of the play goes backward and forward in time as the playwright attempts to fulfill three main arcs of intent. They are:

1.) To show how the plot was planned in advance, including Oswald impersonations.

2.) To show how and why it succeeded, and

3.) To reveal the results of the murder.

Concerning the last, Stanley Marks was one of the first critics to understand that there was a connection between the assassination of President Kennedy and the escalation of the Vietnam War. And this is one of the reasons that the main character King begins to understand that what he had done had unintended consequences. And this is one of the most arresting aspects of the last scenes of the play. In fact, near the end, King has an interesting speech about this:

> Face up to it, Mr. Noslen. Our generation made a mess of it ... By God, if I were in my twenties, I'd be a hippie, at least they are trying to live their lives without using napalm or nuclear weapons. Four-legged animals protect their young; the

two-legged ones compel their young to die for the
benefit of the old.

That theme, of unintended consequences, is foreshadowed
earlier in the play, when King says that he found that a conspiracy is like throwing a stone in the water. The ripples get larger
and more agitated:

Everything those ripples touch reacts in a different
manner. We murdered one man today, but a thousand, no hundreds of thousands are going to die.
No one on this earth well ever be the same.

In addition to that concept about Indochina, Stanley also was
quite aware of another overarching theme that began with
Kennedy's murder and the resultant cover-up. And that was the
ease with which the true conspirators escaped any kind of legal
proceedings for their crimes, and the fact that this created a
signal. The signal was that this crime could be done again, and
again. So the play ends years later as the conspirators walk off
and we hear a woman's voice screaming offstage, "My God, my
God, they've killed him." This clearly suggests the assassination
of Bobby Kennedy.

Rob Couteau has done a good deed in resurrecting and
reviving the works of a valuable man who was all but forgotten.
And thanks indirectly go to Bob Dylan also.

– James DiEugenio

As a scholar and historian, James DiEugenio has devoted many
decades to researching the major Sixties assassinations. The

world's leading authority on the JFK case and the author of *Destiny Betrayed* and *The JFK Assassination*, he's also the screenwriter of Oliver Stone's documentary, *JFK Revisited*. His Kennedys and King website continues to serve as a fundamental source of new research and reviews.

Books by Stanley J. Marks

Since the Markses' works on religion contain a powerful politi-cal dimension, they have also been included here.

The Bear That Walks Like a Man: A Diplomatic and Military Analysis of Soviet Russia (Dorrance and Company, 1943).

History of the U.S. Army and Military Science. (Circa 1945; most likely extant only in manuscript form in a U.S. military archive.)

Murder Most Foul! The Conspiracy That Murdered President Kennedy: 975 Questions & Answers (Los Angeles: Bureau of International Affairs, September 1967).

A Murder Most Foul! Or, A Time to Die; A Time to Cry, described as "A three-act play that reveals how a chief of state was assassinated." Copyrighted February 19, 1968; publication history unknown. A photocopy of this 81-page manuscript was retrieved from the Library of Congress on April 30, 2021. It was rewritten and expanded under the title *A Time to Die, A Time to Cry* (Los Angeles: Bureau of International Affairs, late 1970) and is described as "A three-act play concerning the three murders that changed the course of history: President Kennedy, Martin Luther King, and Senator Robert F. Kennedy." In October 1979 this work was retitled *A Time to Die, A Time to Cry, or, Murders Most Foul!* and was described as "A three-act play relating to the past, present, and future of the figures and events surrounding the murders of President Kennedy, Martin Luther King, and Senator Robert F. Kennedy." (Retrieved from the Copyright Office on April 3, 2021.) Another version of the play was deposited in the Copyright Office in 1988 but has been reported as "lost."

Two Days of Infamy: November 22, 1963; September 28, 1964 (Los Angeles: Bureau of International Affairs, March 1969). "A textbook for government agents, lawyers, professors, and students analyzing the methods of the Warren Commission ... An analytical and legal study."

Coup d'État! Three Murders That Changed the Course of History. President Kennedy, Reverend King, Senator R. F. Kennedy (Los Angeles: Bureau of International Affairs, February 1970).

American Dream, American Nightmare (Los Angeles: Bureau of International Affairs, 1971). Little is known about this book. On March 28, 1979, along with four of Marks' other titles, it was included in the Library of Congress's comprehensive JFK assassination index, *The Assassination of President John F. Kennedy: A Chronological Bibliography*. On the same day, the House of Representatives Select Subcommittee on Assassinations issued its report, which cited these same five assassination-related titles authored by Marks. It's possible that *American Dream, American Nightmare* is simply another version of his assassination play that was later retitled, especially since it doesn't appear in the lists of Marks' book titles that are normally featured on his dust jackets.

Watch What We Do ... Not What We Say! (Los Angeles: Bureau of International Affairs, 1971). "An account of the present trend of the Nixon–Agnew–Mitchell–Southern strategy axis to the possibility of Orwell's '1984' being accomplished by 1972" (from the title page). Also described elsewhere as "guidebook" on Watergate.

Through Distorted Mirrors! The Impact of Monotheism–One God–Upon Modern World Civilization, by Stanley and Ethel Marks (Los Angeles: Bureau of International Affairs, 1972). "A brief history of the Jewish people."

A Time to Die: No Time to Cry! or The Four-hour War A.K.A. World War III (Pasadena, CA: Bureau of International Affairs 1980). "A one-act, two-scene play dealing with reasons why nuclear war is inevitable." Relying "heavily" on documents and statements made by Congressional leaders, the drama is largely a critique of the Carter Doctrine (which justified the use of military force in the Persian Gulf). The play is set entirely in the War Rooms of the Pentagon and Kremlin. The final page of this publication includes a bibliography and a suggestion: "If the world is still 'teetering on the brink,' relax and read something more relaxing." The first book underneath this sentence is Philip Agee's *Inside the Company: CIA Diary*. In the October 1979 version of Marks' play about the assassinations, *A Time to Die, A Time to Cry, or, Murders Most Foul!*, the nucleus of Act III is essentially an earlier rendering of this same play. There it appears under the Act III title: "Armageddon and Apocalypse." Marks must have subsequently realized that Act III worked as a separate, stand-alone dramatic piece.

Three Days of Judgment! by Stanley J. and Ethel Marks (Bureau of International Affairs, March 1981). "A three-act play ... A mystery-detective story, written in the form of a trial, that deals with religion" as well as with the CIA and Vatican politics.

The Two Christs or the Decline and Fall of Christianity, by Stanley J. and Ethel Marks (Los Angeles: Bureau of International Affairs, September 1983). *The Two Christs* is based on secret Vatican documents that became available to the public in 1981, some of which expose the Church's dealings with Mussolini, Franco, and Hitler. The author discusses the establishment of Christianity in the Roman Empire as well as the Reagan–Weinberger doctrine of a preventative nuclear first strike against the USSR. Published in the fall of 1983, Marks also explores the contemporaneous fears of nuclear apocalypse and Armageddon, and the possibility of extermination through the use of nuclear weapons and the widespread use of toxic materials.

Judaism Looks at Christianity, 7 B.C.E.–1986, by Stanley J. and Ethel Marks (San Marino, CA: Bureau of International Affairs, 1986). "A bugle call summoning the American populace to withstand the insidious messages used by the 'reborn' fundamentalist leaders that appeal for a nuclear war against the 'evil empire.'"

A Year in the Lives of the Damned! Reagan, Reaganism, 1986 (San Marino, CA: Bureau of International Affairs, 1988). "The format is written in the form of a diary; each month is a chapter."

Jews Judaism and the United States or the Impact of Judaism upon the American People, by Stanley J. and Ethel M. Marks (San Marino, CA: Bureau of International Affairs, 1990).

Yes, Americans, A Conspiracy Murdered JFK!, by Stanley J. and Ethel M. Marks (San Marino, CA: Bureau of International Affairs, June 1992).

The Defeat, Dishonor, and Disgrace! The Reagan–Bush Regimes: 1981-1993, by Stanley J. Marks (Bureau of International Affairs, 1993).

If This Be Treason...! (San Marino, CA: Bureau of International Affairs, 1996). "The truth of how citizens Reagan, Bush, Casey, and their friends betrayed and destroyed the Carter administration in the 1980 presidential election ... Dedicated to those who seek the spirit of truth and the spirit of freedom."

Justice for Whom? Or, Is Justice for WASPs Only? How the WASP Justice System Worked in Five Trials (Los Angeles: Bureau of International Affairs, 1996). "Five Americans" (including Oswald) "whose criminal or civil trials engaged the attention of millions of people."

Judgment Day! A Play in Three Acts (registered for copyright in 1997; publication history unknown). A play about Judaism. A photocopy of this 198-page manuscript was retrieved from the Copyright Office on April 3, 2021.

Beginning in 1974, the Markses also authored at least five guide books on business and financial investment.

Essays Published by SJM

Review of *One World* by Wendell Willkie. *Chicago Defender*, April 24, 1943, p. 15.

"War and Warfare" weekly column. Nine articles published in the *Chicago Defender*, May 1, 1943–July 10, 1943.

Review of *The Thousand Year Conspiracy* by Paul Winkler. *Chicago Defender*, May 1, 1943, p. 15.

Review of *Germany's Master Plan* by Borkin and Welsh; and *The Coming Showdown* by Carl Dreher. *Chicago Defender*, May 8, 1943, p. 15.

Review of *Between Thunder and the Sun* by Vincent Sheean; and *Jake Home* by Ruth McKenney. *Chicago Defender*, May 15, 1943, p. 15.

Review of *Capricornia* by Xavier Herbert; and *A Latin American Speaks* by Luis Quintanilla. *Chicago Defender*, May 22, 1943, p. 15.

Review of *Round Trip to Russia* by Walter Graebner; and *Free Men of America* by Ezequiel Padilla. *Chicago Defender*, May 29, 1943, p. 15.

Review of *Journey Among Warriors* by Eve Curie. *Chicago Defender*, June 5, 1943, p. 15.

Review of *Brothers Under the Skin* by Carey McWilliams; *Combined Operations: The Official Story of the Commandos* by

Hilary St. George Saunders; and *We Can Win This War* by W. F. Kernan. *Chicago Defender*, June 12, 1943, p. 15.

Review of *The Autobiography of a Curmudgeon* by Harold Ickes. *Chicago Defender*, June 19, 1943, p. 15.

Review of *Moscow Dateline* by Henry C. Cassidy; *Mother Russia* by Maurice Hindus; and *Pursuit of Freedom* by Chicago Civil Liberties Committee. *Chicago Defender*, June 26, 1943, p. 15.

Review of *Attack Can Win in '43* by Max Werner. *Chicago Defender*, July 3, 1943, p. 15.

"An Ode to the Mothers of the 'Chosen People." *California Jewish Voice*, from his feature newspaper column, "All Things Considered." December 31, 1971, p. 15. (Reproduced on p. 306 of SJM's book, *Through Distorted Mirrors!*)

"Allies Kicked by Presidential Political Footwork." *California Jewish Voice*, January 7, 1972, p. 21.

"The Past is the Prologue of the Future." *California Jewish Voice*, January 14, 1972, p. 15.

"Not Only the Land But the Free, Face Menace of Erosion." *California Jewish Voice*, January 28, 1972, p. 11.

Diogenes weekly political newsletter (self-published), 1984, 1988, 1990.

Other books by Stanley Marks
available at DOMINANTSTAR:

Murder Most Foul!
The Conspiracy That Murdered President Kennedy:
975 Questions & Answers

Two Days of Infamy:
November 22, 1963; September 28, 1964

Coup d'Etat!
Three Murders That Changed the Course of History. President
Kennedy, Reverend King, Senator R. F. Kennedy

CPSIA information can be obtained
at www.ICGtesting.com
Printed in the USA
BVHW041117200423
662718BV00015B/558